REAL-TIME BUSINESS INTELLIGENCE MASTERY

CIO'S PLAYBOOK FOR FASTER, SMARTER AI-DRIVEN DECISIONS IN MANUFACTURING

REAL-TIME BUSINESS INTELLIGENCE MASTERY

CIO'S PLAYBOOK FOR FASTER, SMARTER AI-DRIVEN DECISIONS IN MANUFACTURING

Devendra Goyal

Worldwide Published by
Pendown Press

PENDOWN PRESS LLP
An ISO 9001 & ISO 14001 Certified Co.,
Regd. Office: 3767A, Kanhaiya Nagar,
Tri Nagar, Delhi-110035
Ph.: 8130886000, 9650072927, 8595249536
E-mail: info@pendownpress.com
Branch Office: 1A/2A, 20, Hari Sadan, Ansari Road,
Daryaganj, New Delhi-110002
Ph.: 011-45794768
Website: PendownPress.com

Edition: 2024
Price: $9.99/-
ISBN: 978-93-5554-959-4

Layout and Cover Designed by Pendown Graphics Team
Printed and Bound in India by Thomson Press India Ltd.

Dedication

IN LOVING MEMORY OF MY 'DAD'
RAJENDRA GOYAL

CONTENTS

Acknowledgements

First and foremost, huge gratitude to the marketing *"Guru" Akshar Yadav* for introducing me to the wonderful world of marketing.

This book would not have been possible without the sacrifices made by ***My Beautiful Wife Richa and My Lovely Son Ridanssh.***

Also, credit is due to ***My Partner, Manish,*** who has been motivating me to write a book for the last 5 years, and now, finally, it's time to follow his advice.

A heartfelt thank you to all the clients who made me who I am today, it was an honor to serve you.

Finally, a huge hug to ***Pramod and Vaibhav*** who got me into the beautiful world of Data and AI.

I am thankful to my friend Dinesh Verma, CEO, Pendown Press and his team for their support and suggestions throughout the creative process.

Foreword

I have had the pleasure to have met and worked with Dave Goyal over the last 14 years in the field of Business Intelligence transformation and innovation. Throughout our association, I have never been disappointed by the knowledge and technical acumen that he possesses, both in his approach and his overall professionalism in our collective endeavors.

His innate ability to weave in a very mature business knowledge, as well as address critical technological needs clearly and concisely, and to be able to present that in an achievable timeline has been invaluable in my experience with him, and that extends to the personnel he brings in as his team.

With the acceleration of the avalanche of AI innovations that are hitting the market, and impacting all leaders of corporate IT organizations, I am very fortunate to have Dave to consult to help navigate these waters and look forward to continuing our partnership as he assists us in our quest for business growth and IT maturity. He is truly my 'sensei' in all things Data and AI, and I could not be more fortunate and pleased.

The publication of Dave's book on Real-Time BI is poised to further cement his influence in the industry. It promises to be a pivotal resource, offering insights and methodologies that can transform how organizations approach data analysis and decision-making in real-time scenarios. This book is expected to set new standards in BI practices, enabling organizations to leverage real-time data analytics for enhanced decision-making, operational efficiency, and competitive advantage. Dave's legacy as a luminary in the BI domain will undoubtedly be shaping future trends in business intelligence and analytics.

Finally, I must say that beyond all the capabilities that Dave possesses at a professional level, his humility, his quiet demeanor, and his caring, stand out as differentiators in this world of promise makers and marketers. He is simply stated, a quality human being whom I am so very grateful to be able to call more than a business colleague, but a friend.

Claudé E Zamboni

VP, IT

QSC Audio

Preface

Over the course of my extensive 30-year journey into the somewhat enigmatic world of Data and AI, I encountered two primary obstacles.

- Inaccuracy of the reported data.
- Delayed business insights, thus impeding timely decision-making.

I was considering penning a book aimed at Demystifying Data and AI when Ryan, a long-term client turned close friend, put forth a question.

He asked, "Dave, you have ample experience in Data and AI solutions. Are you aware of or have implemented a Real-Time Business Intelligence Solution?".

This prompted me to ponder. Conventionally, Business Intelligence Solutions necessitate a Data Warehouse implementation, serving as the singular data source for Business Intelligence to garner immediate insights and make choices.

However, the issue lies in the time-consuming data synchronization process, resulting in an approximate 1-day lag. Hence, your insights are rendered obsolete by a day.

This may seem manageable for some businesses but poses a serious hindrance for manufacturers and medical device organizations.

This book serves as the culmination of my three-decade-long journey into the mystical world of Data and AI, predominantly for Manufacturing firms. Manufacturers and Medical Device organizations continually face difficulties in obtaining timely and correct data insights crucial for accurate decision-making.

The book further encompasses my time spent assisting and transforming Manufacturing corporations' CIOs, CTOs, CFOs, COOs, and industry intellectuals, offering a non-technical perspective. Additionally, it assists in comprehending the prerequisites to launch a successful Business Intelligence initiative without incurring exorbitant expenses.

Through adherence to our strategy and roadmap, we have launched over 50 of these solutions, each rendering a tenfold return on the investment.

About Me

Before you flip the pages to the transformative content in the book, I am sure you would be curious to know who is behind this book. So, here's a peek into my life and work.

While growing up, I was always fascinated and driven towards creating innovations and profitable ventures. From running a guitar tutoring shop for kids to helping a friend secure a loan for his organic chemical factory, to finally creating a world-class Data and AI software solutions company. I've had 9 ventures in my journey with a fair share of failure and success and making so many friends along the way.

I've learned from my mistakes, from naive beginnings to trial and error, to finally owning and founding an ever-growing organization.

My initial experience is in developing custom web applications, enterprise solutions and complex solutions using technologies like C, C++, Java, C#, SharePoint and SQL Server and several cross-platform libraries for Linux, Mac OS, and Windows OS.

I was part of the Microsoft AI-inner circle. "Think AI Consulting Corporation", the company I co-founded with my friend and partner Manish Bhardia, is a Microsoft

Solution Partner and "Data and AI" space previously named as "Gold Competency Partner".

I am a serial entrepreneur and co-founded 3 more companies namely "Think AI India Consulting", "BI Demantra" and "Orange Neurosciences".

I also own a US Patent for a Neuro Disease which is novel in its category.

I am also the "Top Voice" in "Business Intelligence" and "Data Warehouse" on LinkedIn and publish a weekly newsletter called "Demystify Data and AI".

For the last 30 years, I have been extensively working in strategizing and implementing Artificial Intelligence, Business Intelligence and Data warehousing solutions for manufacturing and healthcare organizations.

Testimonial

TRANSFORMING DATA INTO INSIGHTS

I would like to extend my sincere appreciation for the exceptional work done by Dave Goyal in our collaboration with Impedimed. Dave's expertise in data modeling, combined with his profound understanding of business requirements, was pivotal in delivering a high-quality Data Warehouse & Business Intelligence solution for our SOZO Analytics.

His ability to navigate complex data landscapes & translate them into actionable insights has greatly benefited our project, ensuring a seamless experience for our customers from within our app. Dave's dedication to excellence and his capacity to deliver on promises truly set him apart in the field of Data & AI consultancy.

Shashi Tripati

Chief Operating Officer

Testimonial

A MENTOR'S PERSPECTIVE

I have had the pleasure of knowing Dave for more than 2 decades and worked with him closely for several years. During this time, his eagerness to acquire new knowledge has been truly remarkable.

In a brief period, Dave mastered the intricacies of BI and DW through Cognos, transitioning seamlessly from a .NET architect to a BI Architect with impressive speed. Having had the chance to mentor him, I am thrilled to witness his rapid growth and am excited for what the future holds for him.

Pramod Kunju

President and CEO

Testimonial

TRUSTED THOUGHT PARTNERS

My association with Dave Goyal goes back to over 12 years ago when he was the lead technical manager on a Business Intelligence effort that company was undertaking. I found him very knowledgeable, amiable to suggestions and technical astute in both his approach and his coordination of the effort. I was so impressed with his acumen in architecting an enterprising reporting ecosystem for the business. In that time, Dave created a new company, Think AI, that we engaged with and relied on for technical augmentation resources, and strategic planning and direction. They have become trusted thought partners as we navigate the nuances of the needs of our business.

Dave has been, and will continue to be, a vital resource for us as we evolve our enterprise environment to provide vital up-to-the-minute information to our constituents to guide our business growth and maturity.

Claude E Zamboni

Vice President, Information Technology

Testimonial

FINGERS ON THE PULSE OF INDUSTRY TRENDS

Dave Goyal is a preeminent B.I. technologist who has the rare ability to see into the future. In a rapidly changing technical landscape, Dave has his finger on the pulse of the industry and is able to identify technical trends that are shaping the future of data analytics and artificial intelligence.

In his clear and concise writing. Dave leverages his unique skills to convey how cutting-edge technologies can be leveraged to solve real-world business problems.

Ryan Mohrman

IT Director, Enterprise Architecture

Testimonial

NARROWING DOWN POSSIBILITIES

I have had the pleasure of working with Dave Goyal for over a decade on Microsoft BI Solutions & technology road mapping for my medical device company. When it comes to strategy, Dave is invaluable to our organization as he understands so well what's possible but also can help us narrow down possibilities into practical applications of technology. As a forward-thinking leader, Dave has navigated our organization through the ever evolving landscape of Microsoft technologies.

His strategic vision aligns seamlessly with Microsoft's roadmap, ensuring that we stay relevant. From Azure to Power BI, Dave has guided us toward innovative solutions that drive efficiency & growth. The team he has put together is an integral part of our day-to-day operations making our BI vision come to life.

Gabrielle Carr

Vice President FP&A and Sales Operations

Testimonial

EMPOWERING DATA-DRIVEN DECISIONS

Dave Goyal has been a key partner for St. John's for over 10 years, and I have had the unique privilege of working with him directly for the past three years. It is rare to find a collaborative partner with such a deep level of technical expertise related to Business Intelligence best practices who Also demonstrates such profound business acumen and wisdom.

Dave and his team have facilitated a great partnership which has allowed St. John's to transform our decision making processes through actionable insights. It has been a unique privilege to work with such a stellar person on this journey.

Sharon Marie Correa

Chief Information Officer

Testimonial

STRONG CONSULTATIVE APPROACH

Dave and his firm is dedicated to deep business intelligence expertise, a strong knowledge of database architecture and query language, as well as intensive reporting best practices. BI Demantra displayed a strong command of the relevant Business Intelligence tools available in the market.

They take a strongly consultative approach to advising their customers, putting the customer needs & aspirations in the forefront. I can always count on Dave to be knowledgeable, responsive & committed to our client's success.

Lori Seal

Chief Operating Officer

Why Does This Book Matter?

The importance of this book cannot be overstated given the ever-evolving advancements in Business Intelligence and Analytics using AI. In this rapidly changing landscape, Data and AI have emerged as the game changer for success. This is significantly apparent in manufacturing industries, where decision-making speed and accuracy can significantly influence profit margins.

This book will play a crucial role in bridging the gap between technical potential and practical, lucrative outcomes for predicting business success in the manufacturing world.

- **A Glimpse Through the Insider's Lens:** The book offers exceptional perspectives from an industry expert with a three-decade-long journey in the Data and AI world. It encapsulates years of practical experience solving real-life problems, revealing fascinating insights into the challenges and victories involved when implementing Business Intelligence solutions.

- **Simplifying C-Level Dialogues:** With a focus on everyday language, the book effectively acts as a critical link between intricate data ideas and executive professionals making strategic choices. It communicates directly to CIOs, CTOs, CFOs, and COOs, simplifying technical terms and proposing comprehensive intelligence.
- **Emphasizing Practical and Profitable Intelligence:** The book stresses on the importance of investment returns, highlighting more than 65 instances where the appropriate strategy and direction in Business Intelligence yielded stellar returns. These demonstrated scenarios represent practical solutions with measurable results, not just theoretical constructs.
- **Handling Data Challenges:** Addressing the ongoing issues of precision and speed in data reporting, the book outlines creative strategies to counter them and emphasizes the importance of timely and trustworthy data reporting for business triumph.
- **The Question that Ignited a Revolution:** The book's story begins with a question from a longtime customer, representing a journey for a solution that can negate the inherent delays of conventional data

warehousing. This pursuit unraveled revelations and solutions crucial for manufacturers who can't afford even a day's delay in insights.

- **Exploring the Latest Findings:** The book telescopes beyond traditional Business Intelligence, intruding into the territory of Real-Time Business Intelligence and AI. It empowers readers to understand the inadequacies of the market options and how to surpass this limitation and avoid costly mistakes while still maintaining a competitive edge.
- **A Step-by-Step Guide:** The book serves as an expert course in devising a strategy and flows as a 5-Step Playbook that employs Real Time BI and Analytics strategies, offers frameworks for selecting the appropriate team and tools, and proves that investments in data are profit-earning and not mere spending.
- **Highlighting Data and AI as a Future Success Indicator:** The book emphasizes the role of Data and AI as a future success forecaster and readies leaders with the aptitude to not only decipher data for immediate gains but also predict and pivot future market trends and growth prospects.

In summary, **"Real Time Business Intelligence Mastery"** is more than a playbook or a guide; it's a manifesto for those who understand the need for Data and AI solutions but haven't completely utilized it yet. It sends out a strong message for manufacturing firms aiming to flourish in an AI-driven Data culture.

Introduction

THE NEW ERA OF DATA-DRIVEN DECISIONS

The name of my own story is **"Connecting the Dots."**

Imagine a manufacturing company at a critical turning point, ready to make a big move in the competitive world of business. Adopting real-time business intelligence (BI) strategies drove it from obscurity to market leader, turning data into gold.

This is not just their story—it's the future for any business ready to embrace the Real-Time Business Intelligence revolution.

➤ The Importance of Real-Time BI

In the age of information, understanding BI is a must-have to get the most out of data systems such as IOTs, Devices, ERP, CRM, and line of business systems.

- **Understanding BI and Its Impact:** BI isn't just about crunching numbers; it's about crafting narratives from data streams. It aids in finding and discovering patterns for smarter insights and provides a guide for better decision-making.
- **The Evolution of BI in the Digital Age:** As technology gallops forward, BI has evolved from rear-view mirror hindsight to the high-beam

foresight of real-time analytics. With the growth of AI, it's no longer a reference system but rather a driver for each organization to grow their business in the competitive age and get faster results.

- **Key Benefits of Adopting Real-Time BI:** Real-time Business Intelligence (BI) isn't just about getting data faster. It's like having a crystal ball for your business. It helps you see trends and make quick decisions, so you can keep up with what your customers want and stay ahead of the competition. It's all about being able to look ahead and change things up as you go, keeping your business sharp and competitive.

➢ Why This Book?

In the midst of confusing terminology and complicated theories, this book acts as an inspiration, leading you towards achieving mastery in Real-Time Business Intelligence.

- **CIO's Toolkit:** If you're a Technology Leader keen on leveraging the latest technology to boost your business and earn your stakeholders' trust, this book is tailored for you.
- **Unique Approach of the 5-Step Playbook:** This playbook is your BI compass, pointing the way to insightful, swift decision-making.

- **Focus on Cost-Effectiveness and Speed:** Unlock the secrets of executing BI strategies that don't break the bank but do break the mold.
- **Tailored for Small to Midsize Businesses:** Whether you're a startup or an established organization, these strategies are designed for you.

➢ What to Expect

Let's lay out the map and mark the milestones of your journey through the playbook.

- **Overview of the Chapters:** Each chapter unfolds a step of the playbook, a strategic move in the grand game of Real-Time BI.
- **How to Apply the Playbook to Your Business:** Translate the steps into action, molding the strategies to fit the contours of your unique business landscape.

As we turn the page on the prelude to your BI adventure, remember that the power of Real-Time BI is within reach. This introduction has set the stage for a transformative journey—one where data isn't just processed, but harnessed; decisions aren't just made, but informed; and businesses don't just compete, but lead.

Points to Remember

- Real-time BI is about making decisions that are as dynamic as the market itself.
- The evolution of BI has turned data into the most valuable currency in the digital economy.
- This book is a blueprint for those who aspire to weave data into the fabric of their decision-making process.

- Now that you understand the power of real-time BI, let's dive into the first step of the playbook.
- With the scene set and the cast ready, your story of transformation begins. Prepare to embark on a journey that will navigate the intricacies of Real Time Business Intelligence (BI), steering your business towards uncharted territories of success.

Part I

BUILDING THE FOUNDATION

Chapter-1

Laying the Groundwork for Real-Time Business Intelligence

Did you know that nearly 60% of business decisions made by companies take too long to be effective? In a landscape where speed and precision are the keystones of success, this is more than a statistic; it's a call for transformation.

This chapter is about taking that first crucial leap into the world of Real-Time Business Intelligence (BI) - an essential step towards smarter, faster business decisions.

Let's first understand the building blocks of a true Business Intelligence system where a Data warehouse serves as the central repository and single version of truth.

The diagram illustrates a comprehensive Business Intelligence and Data Warehousing system, encompassing the flow from various data sources to actionable insights.

It begins with a range of data sources including structured data coming from Enterprise Resource Planning

(ERP) systems, Customer Relationship Management (CRM) platforms, Supply Chain Management (SCM), Manufacturing Execution Systems (MES), Lines of Business (LOB) applications; or unstructured data such as Internet of Things (IoT) devices, and diverse file types such as Excel and flat files. These disparate sources are then funneled through an ETL (Extraction, Transformation, Loading) process, which is pivotal in consolidating, cleaning, and structuring the data for storage and analysis. The processed data is stored in a Data Warehouse, which could be segmented into Metadata, Summary Data, and Raw Data to support varied analytical needs and maintain data integrity.

The Data Warehouse then serves as the central repository for Self-Serve platforms for on-demand access, Reporting tools for structured output, Alert systems for proactive issue detection, and Data Science for advanced analytical processes. Each of these applications serves a distinct purpose, transforming raw data into strategic insights.

Additionally, underpinning the entire system is a layer of Security, Compliance, Audit, DevOps, and Change Management protocols to ensure that data governance is maintained and the system operates within the required regulatory frameworks. This architecture not only secures the data but also provides a robust foundation for agile development and efficient management of the data lifecycle.

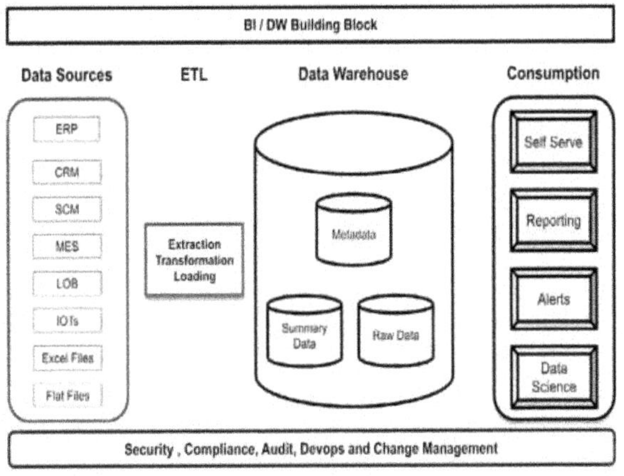

1. Understanding Your Data

Envision data as individual pixels that come together to form a full image on a display. It's key to making smart choices. Now, let's use the image of Business Intelligence (BI) to make pixels of data less complicated.

Types of Data Relevant to Business Intelligence:

Before we progress further, it's important to grasp the kinds of data that can be gathered.

- **Structured Data:** Clear and well-organized, structured data is the backbone of any BI system, providing the straightforward insights needed for rapid decision-making.
- **Unstructured Data:** Imagine the raw narratives from customer feedback or the chaotic symphony

of machine sensors - this is where hidden gems of insight lie, waiting to be discovered.

- **Semi-Structured Data:** Residing between chaos and order, semi-structured data like JSON or EDI transactions combines elements of both, offering a flexible medium for BI.

With an array of sources ranging from the inner workings of your business databases to the wide-reaching arms of social media, each type of data brings its unique brushstrokes to the overall picture of your business operations.

2. The Importance of Data Quality

Consider the impact of a mislabeled location on a map - suddenly, you're not where you think you are. In industries like medical device manufacturing, poor data quality can inflate costs by 20% due to recalls and compliance failures. It's not just about speed; it's about steering your BI with the compass of reliability and precision.

- Efficient Data Collection

  The technique of gathering data is continuously improving. Where once data was slowly and laboriously entered by hand, much like the meticulous work of chiseling stone, we now see the automation of data collection as the quick and precise turning of the sculptor's wheel, handling large volumes of data with ease. Thanks to technologies like APIs, systems integration, and the real-time data-gathering capabilities of IoT devices, we are advancing towards a scenario where data is not merely amassed but also refined and prepared for immediate use.

3. Choosing the Right Tools

Selecting the right BI tool is less about choosing a weapon and more about finding the right key to unlock the potential of your business's data.

➤ An Overview of BI Tools on the Market

In the diverse ecosystem of BI tools, stalwarts like Tableau, Power BI, Sisense, Domo, and Alteryx are the foundational pillars, offering robust analytics and in-depth visualization to navigate the complexities of large datasets. They are seasoned guides in the BI terrain, capable of driving strategic decisions with a breadth of capabilities.

On the other end, Looker and Qlik emerge as the fine-tuned instruments of the BI orchestra, conducting data into harmonies of insight with their intuitive platforms and adaptable frameworks. They're the artisans of data analytics, painting a detailed picture of business trends and patterns.

However, the landscape still has uncharted territories, particularly in seamlessly integrating real-time data with traditional BI tools. While some tools adeptly process live data, the maze of technical setup and maintenance can be daunting. Moreover, there's a burgeoning need for tools that not only analyze but also automate decision-making based on real-time insights – a gap that is only now beginning to close.

- Evaluating Tools Based on Cost and Features

  In a world where not all treasuries are overflowing, evaluating BI tools is a delicate balance between cost and functionality. It's about finding the right fit that aligns with both your strategic needs and your purse strings.

- Custom Solutions vs. Off-the-Shelf Software

  Sometimes, the journey calls for a custom-crafted solution – a system so in tune with your business that it feels like an extension of your own thought process. Yet, such tailored solutions come with their own set of challenges, including cost and implementation timelines. Off-the-shelf software, while not as personalized, offers a ready-made entry point into the world of BI, often with the flexibility to adapt to a variety of scenarios.

4. Building a Data-Driven Culture

Creating a data-driven culture isn't about rallying a crew; it's about inspiring every individual to become a navigator in the BI odyssey.

- Methods for Cultivating Acceptance

  The path towards a culture that values data starts when leaders take the initiative to guide, use success stories to light the way, and use distinct, quantifiable goals to track advancements.

- Training and Development for Your Team

  Providing Business Intelligence training is similar to giving explorers the ability to navigate by the stars. A team that has received comprehensive training can confidently traverse the vast oceans of data.

- Overcoming Resistance to Change

  Change is the great ocean all businesses must cross. It requires showing the crew the wonders that lie across the sea of data, supported by continuous encouragement, clear communication, and collective involvement in the journey.

Δ Summary

In this chapter, we've laid out the foundation for Real-Time Business Intelligence. We've learned to identify and classify the various forms of data that pulse through the veins of our businesses. We've recognized the value of data quality, not just for its ability to inform but also to steer clear of costly errors. We've explored the modern mechanisms of data collection, which promise not just to gather but to refine and ready our data for real-time action. We've navigated the varied landscape of BI tools, weighing their capabilities against the scales of our needs and resources. And lastly, we've sown the seeds of a data-driven culture, fertile ground for growth and innovation.

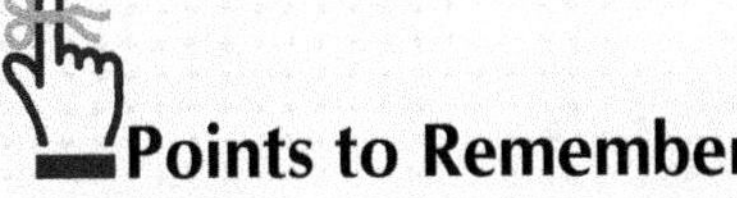

- Data is the currency of decision-making; treat it with the respect it deserves.
- Clean, quality data is not a luxury—it's a necessity for precision and performance.
- The right BI tool for your business should feel like a natural extension of your strategy, fitting your needs and budget.
- Cultivating a data-driven culture is a collective voyage that begins with leadership and is embraced by all.
- Embrace change as an ally; your adaptability defines your future success.

- With a solid foundation in place, let's explore how to transform data into actionable insights.
- This pivotal sentence bridges our foundational understanding of BI data to the thrilling prospects ahead—turning raw data into strategic gold.

Chapter-2

From Data to Decisions: The Analysis Process

What if you had the insight to anticipate market shifts before they occurred? Imagine harnessing the clarity to foresee opportunities and navigate the complexities of business with the confidence of an expert strategist. This chapter is your guide, to transforming the mystery of data into clear-cut decisions.

Let's first understand the Data to Decisions life cycle:

- **Gather Data:** Collect relevant data from various sources.
- **Define KPIs:** Identify Key Performance Indicators that will help measure success.
- **Visualize Data:** Create visual representations of data to identify patterns and trends.
- **Actionable Insights:** Derive meaningful insights from the visualized data that can inform business decisions.

- **Prioritize Decisions:** Determine which actions to take based on the insights gained, ranking them by importance and impact.
- **Execute:** Implement the decisions that have been prioritized to achieve desired outcomes.
- **Monitor:** Continuously observe the results of the executed actions, adjusting strategies as needed.

Note: The process is surrounded by a feedback loop, indicating that it is iterative and cyclical, with monitoring leading back to the data-gathering stage to begin the cycle anew.

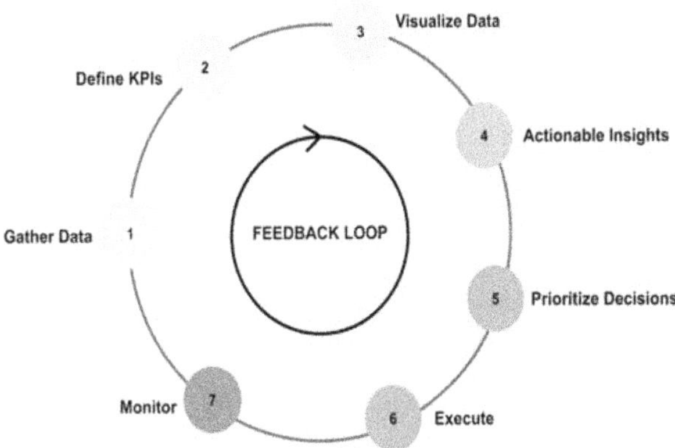

Let's explore the details of each step here:

1. Data Processing and Cleaning

In the intricate dance of data-driven manufacturing, the initial step is to ensure that our data—the lifeblood of our operations—is pure and precise. Similar to prepping a high-performance engine, we start by refining our data for the journey ahead.

Δ *Ensuring Data Purity*

Ensuring data purity is pivotal for precision in manufacturing analytics. It's about implementing rigorous data cleaning protocols and leveraging sophisticated automated tools to refine and distill data. This process, exactly like quality control in production, ensures that every decision is informed by data that is as flawless and reliable as the products rolling off the assembly line.

Δ *The Importance of Cleaning Data*

In the digital fabric of today's manufacturing, data stands as the foundation. It's imperative to maintain data cleanliness to achieve a crystal-clear view of operations. This clarity isn't just about aesthetics; it's about functionality. Clean data leads to precise analytics, which in turn leads to decisions that can be made with confidence and exactitude. It's the difference between a blurry photograph and a high-definition image; the latter allows for informed decisions, where every pixel counts.

Δ *Automated Tools for Data Processing*

In the toolkit of a modern manufacturer, automated data processing tools are indispensable. These tools don't just remove redundancies and errors; they enhance the quality of the data. They are essential for distilling the data down to its most informative elements, ensuring that the insights you derive are based on the most accurate and up-to-date information available.

For technology leaders, the call to action is clear:

- Invest in automated tools to elevate your data quality.
- Train your teams to use them effectively.
- Integrate data quality tools into your daily operations to maintain the highest standard of data integrity.

With this approach, you create a manufacturing environment that reflects the precision of your data—a system where excellence is not an aspiration, but a given, and every decision is informed by data that's as accurate and reliable as the machinery on your factory floor.

2. Analyzing Data for Insights

With clean data now in hand, we stand at the threshold of discovery for deep insights that will illuminate the path forward. This is the moment where data transforms from raw numbers into a strategic compass, guiding us through the complex terrain of manufacturing with clarity and foresight.

Δ *Techniques for Data Analysis*

In the arsenal of data analysis, each technique serves as a strategic asset, unveiling the concealed patterns and actionable insights nestled within complex data. Here's how to mobilize these techniques effectively:

In the realm of real-time business intelligence (BI), the application of generative AI involves employing artificial intelligence algorithms capable of creating new data or materials by analyzing patterns and insights from existing datasets. This feature paves the way for innovative approaches to bolster business intelligence, offering real-time insights, forecasts, and practical advice.

Here are some ways generative AI can be utilized within real-time business intelligence:

- Retrieval-Augmented Generation (RAG):

  Retrieval-Augmented Generation (RAG) merges information retrieval with generative AI to deliver precise, context-aware insights for real-time business intelligence (BI). By smoothly mining relevant data from extensive business databases and generating informed responses, RAG enables businesses to tackle complex queries with nuanced, actionable intelligence. Its capacity to adapt to dynamic market conditions and inform decision-making processes in real time makes it a pivotal asset for businesses aiming to maintain a competitive edge through enhanced operations and customer engagement. Let's see an example of this later.

➢ Utilizing Generative AI for Predictive Analytics

- **Forecasting Time Series Data:** Generative algorithms are adept at projecting upcoming trends and data patterns over time, such as forecasting sales, predicting consumer demand, or estimating inventory levels, which empowers companies to make well-informed choices.
- **Identifying Anomalies:** AI has the knack for spotting irregular patterns or anomalies within live data feeds, providing businesses with immediate alerts to potential risks or chances.
- **Deploy AI Models:** Integrate advanced AI models to scrutinize your data, uncovering predictive patterns that forecast market trends and customer preferences. This is not just about reacting to the present; it's about preempting the future and equipping your business with the power to anticipate and adapt.
- **Refine Predictive Algorithms:** Continuously train and refine your predictive algorithms to increase their accuracy. Use them to conduct what-if

scenarios, ensuring your manufacturing operations can quickly adapt to potential changes in the supply chain or consumer demand.

- Natural Language Generation (NLG)
    - **Real-Time Report Generation:** Generative AI is capable of drafting reports that summarize critical business metrics and insights derived from data, continuously updating these reports as fresh data becomes available.
    - **Enhancing Customer Interactions:** AI-driven chatbots and virtual assistants can craft responses that mimic human interaction in real time, thus enhancing customer service and involvement.
- Generative Design
    - **Advancing Product Development:** AI can generate a plethora of design options based on specific requirements or limits, accelerating the pace of innovation, and reducing the time it takes to launch a product.
    - **Optimizing Processes:** Through simulating various scenarios, generative AI can recommend improvements to business operations, logistics, and supply chain management.

- Synthetic Data Generation
  - **Safeguarding Data Privacy:** Generative AI is able to produce synthetic datasets that resemble real data, which allows for the analysis and sharing of confidential or regulated data without disclosing the actual data.
  - **Expanding Data for Training:** When the available data is insufficient, generative models can create additional data points to enhance the training of models and boost the accuracy of forecasts.
- Decision Support Systems
  - **Strategic Scenario Planning:** Generative AI models can forecast a range of business scenarios using current data trends and external influences, supporting strategic planning, and managing risks.
  - **Enhancing Decision Making:** AI can suggest the most advantageous decisions or actions to improve business outcomes, including devising pricing strategies, managing inventory, or allocating resources efficiently.

Δ *Implementation Considerations*

Deploying generative AI in real-time business intelligence necessitates a thorough evaluation of data infrastructure, selecting appropriate models, and persistent monitoring for ethical usage and model efficacy. Integration with pre-existing BI tools and systems is essential for smooth operation and widespread acceptance. Additionally, it's critical for enterprises to consider the ethical implications and potential biases in generative AI models to guarantee their fair and responsible deployment.

By facilitating the automation of analysis, generation of insights, and enhancement of decision-making processes, generative AI holds the promise to significantly improve real-time business intelligence, thereby enabling businesses to become more agile and well-informed in their operations.

Δ *Mastering Data Visualization for Clarity*

- Implement Visualization Tools: Adopt cutting-edge data visualization tools that can convert complex data points into comprehensible and interactive dashboards. These visual stories should not only inform but also engage stakeholders at all levels, fostering a data-driven culture across your organization.
- Customize Dashboards for Various Functions: Tailor your data visualizations to suit different departmental needs, from the production line to the C-suite, ensuring that each team has access to relevant, real-time data that informs their specific operational decisions.

By embracing these analytical techniques and continuously honing them, you transform data from an abstract concept into a tangible strategic guide, leading to more informed, data-driven decision-making throughout the manufacturing process.

3. Making Data-Driven Decisions

The art of making data-driven decisions lies in the ability to translate analysis into action. It's about reading between the lines of data to uncover the true narrative of what's driving your manufacturing processes.

➢ How to Interpret Analysis Results

- **Develop Data Analysis Expertise:** Ensure your team can interpret data with the same expertise as reading a technical blueprint. Provide training that focuses on understanding data analytics, enabling team members to identify trends, outliers, and patterns that signal both opportunities and threats.
- **Craft Action Plans Based on Data:** Use the insights gained from data interpretation to create actionable strategies. For instance, if data shows a bottleneck in production, develop a targeted plan to address the specific stage causing delays.

- Avoiding Common Pitfalls in Decision-Making
  - **Promote Data-Led Culture:** Cultivate an environment where decisions are made based on data, not intuition, to avoid cognitive biases. Encourage teams to question assumptions and validate them against hard data.
  - **Implement Checks and Balances:** Establish a review process where strategic decisions are evaluated against data insights by multiple stakeholders, which helps prevent overthinking and ensures diverse perspectives are considered.
- Improve with an iterative approach
  - **Share and Learn from Success Stories:** Regularly share case studies within the organization that showcase the successful application of data-driven decisions, such as a product line revamp that led to increased market share due to changes informed by customer data analytics.
  - **Incentivize Successful Data Utilization:** Recognize and reward departments or individuals who effectively use data to drive significant business results, reinforcing the value of a data-driven approach.

By embracing these strategies, you empower your organization to make informed decisions that are backed by data, driving efficiency and innovation in the manufacturing process.

4. Example:

Real-Time Production Optimization in Manufacturing

Consider a manufacturing company that operates in a highly competitive and rapidly changing market. The company seeks to optimize its production line in real time, responding dynamically to fluctuations in demand, supply chain disruptions, and changes in manufacturing conditions. Here's how a Retrieval-Augmented Generation (RAG) system could be applied:

The company deploys a RAG system integrated with its business intelligence platform. This system has access to a vast database of historical production data, market trends, supply chain updates, and real-time IoT sensor data from the manufacturing floor.

Δ Situation

A sudden spike in demand for one of the company's key products is detected, coupled with a delay in the supply of a critical component due to a disruption in the supply chain.

Δ Solution

- ➢ RAG Application:
  - **Retrieval Phase:** The RAG system quickly retrieves relevant historical data on previous demand spikes, supply chain disruptions, and their impacts

on production. It also pulls in real-time data from the production line sensors and external market trend analyses.

- **Generation Phase:** Using this retrieved information, the RAG model generates several optimized production plans. These plans consider various factors, such as adjusting production schedules to prioritize the high-demand product, reallocating resources from less critical products, and identifying alternative suppliers or components to mitigate supply chain issues.

Δ Outcome

The system then presents these optimized production plans to the company's decision-makers, complete with projections on outcomes, potential bottlenecks, and recommendations on the most efficient use of resources. This enables the company to make informed decisions quickly, adapting its production line to meet market demand while minimizing disruptions and costs.

This example illustrates the power of RAG in manufacturing, where it leverages both historical and real-time data to generate actionable insights. By doing so, it helps the company remain agile, responsive to market conditions, and maintain a competitive edge through optimized operations.

∆ Summary

In this chapter, we've navigated the transformative process of turning raw data into valuable insights. We have learned the modern techniques to implement Real-Time Business Intelligence e.g. RAG or Predictive Analytics. We've armed ourselves with the tools and wisdom to cleanse, analyze, and apply data in ways that chart a course toward informed and effective decision-making.

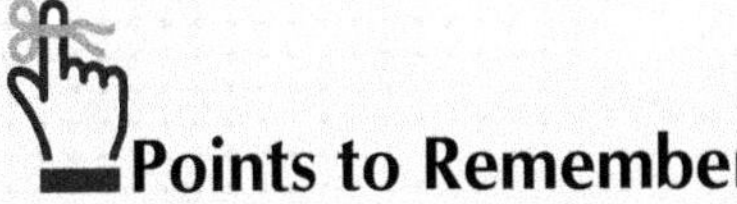

Points to Remember

- Clean, high-quality data is the foundation of sound analysis; it's the starting point of our journey.
- Embrace automated tools and modern Generative AI techniques as trusted allies in processing and predicting the data landscape.
- Visualization is our compass, guiding us through the complexities of data with clarity and ease.
- The art of decision-making combines the boldness to act on data's guidance with the prudence to sidestep common analytical traps.

"Now that you've made your decisions, how do you implement them efficiently?"

As we transition from the realm of analysis, we prepare to delve into the world of action. Our next chapter "Integrating Real-Time Data Streams" is the first step in our playbook. It promises to explore the integration of real-time data streams, ensuring that the decisions we make are not only insightful but also timely, keeping pace with the ever-evolving world of business.

Part II

THE 5-STEP PLAYBOOK

Chapter-3

STEP 1 - Integrating Real-Time Data Streams

In the busy world of manufacturing, there is a client of ours constantly struggling against the dragon of downtime, a relentless force eating away time and resources. This story unfolds how they turned to the power of real-time data, creating a potent tool that vanquished downtime, dramatically enhancing efficiency, and driving the company to outstanding levels of productivity.

To simplify this process, we have a 5-step process in this playbook. Let's first understand those steps before deep diving into "Integration"

- **Integrate:** Combine data from diverse sources to create a unified view.
- **Visualize:** Represent data graphically to facilitate understanding and insight.
- **Automate:** Employ technology to perform repetitive data tasks efficiently.

- **Execute:** Put plans into action based on data-driven strategies.
- **Data Culture:** Foster an organizational culture that values and utilizes data in decision-making.

The central idea of this playbook is an Iterative Approach, suggesting that each of these steps is part of a continuous process of improvement and refinement.

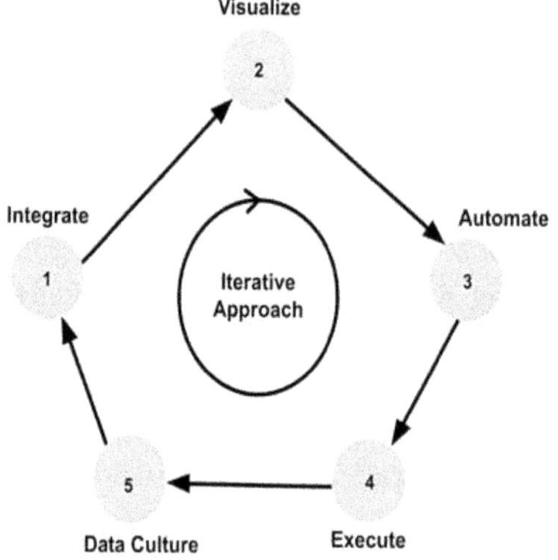

As you can imagine, "Integrating Real-Time Data Streams" is the cornerstone to start the journey into the world of "Real-Time BI" or "Real-Time Decision-Making System".Here are the steps to integrate Real-Time Data Streams.

1. Identifying Key Data Sources

The first step in crafting this mighty sword was to gather the finest materials—data from the most reliable sources.

- ERP Systems

  Harness the pulse of your production floor with real-time data from ERP systems, capturing everything from inventory levels to workflow efficiencies.

- CRM Platforms

  Tap into live customer interactions through CRM data, understanding client needs and market trends as they unfold.

  The voice of the customers guides the company on what products are favored and where improvements can be made.

- IoT Sensors

  IoT sensors are your eyes and ears on the ground, providing instant updates on equipment status and environmental conditions.

- Social Media Feeds

  Real-time social media analytics offer a window into consumer sentiment and emerging market shifts, directly from the digital voice of the public.

- **Supply Chain Trackers**

  Keep a finger on the pulse of your supply chain with trackers that report the live status of materials from source to production line.

- **Financial Software**

  Financial software streams give you a real-time ledger of your fiscal health, from cash flow to expenditures, fueling financially savvy decisions.

- **Machine Telemetry**

  Machine telemetry data provides a continuous stream of performance metrics, enabling proactive maintenance and efficiency optimizations.

- **Quality Control Systems**

  Instant quality checks from control systems mean you can maintain excellence in production with minimal lag time.

- **Employee Performance Monitors**

  Real-time data on employee performance and operations allows for on-the-spot management and productivity boosts.

- **Market Data Services**

  Stay ahead of the curve by integrating live market data services for a strategic edge in pricing, demand forecasting, and competitive analysis.

2. Streamlining Data Integration

Integrating data from various sources into a cohesive real-time business intelligence (BI) solution requires a strategic approach to ensure seamless flow and utility.

Here's how to streamline data integration from the mentioned sources:

- ERP Systems
  - **Automate Data Extraction:** Implement ETL (Extract, Transform, Load) processes to automate data extraction, ensuring ERP data flows continuously into your BI tools.
  - **Standardize Data Formats:** Standardize ERP data formats for compatibility with your BI solution, facilitating smoother integration and analysis.
- CRM Platforms
  - **API Integration:** Utilize APIs to directly integrate CRM platforms with your BI system, allowing for real-time customer data analytics.
  - **Data Syncing:** Ensure regular syncing between CRM and BI tools to maintain up-to-date customer insights across platforms.
- IoT Sensors
  - **Stream Processing:** Deploy stream processing technologies to handle IoT data in real time,

enabling immediate insights into equipment status and environmental conditions.

- **Edge Computing:** Use edge computing to preprocess data at or near the source, reducing latency and bandwidth use before sending it to your BI system.

➤ Social Media Feeds

- **Social Media Aggregators:** Employ social media aggregators to compile and standardize data from various platforms for easier integration into your BI solution.
- **Sentiment Analysis Tools:** Integrate sentiment analysis tools to automatically categorize and quantify social media data for immediate insights.

➤ Supply Chain Trackers

- **Cloud-Based Integration:** Leverage cloud-based platforms for integrating supply chain tracker data, ensuring scalability and accessibility.
- **Real-Time Dashboards:** Develop real-time dashboards that display supply chain status updates directly from trackers to BI tools for instant decision-making.

➤ Financial Software

- **Direct Data Feeds:** Establish direct data feeds between financial software and BI systems for real-time financial analytics.

- **Data Mapping:** Map financial data fields to BI models to ensure accurate representation and analysis of financial health.

➢ Machine Telemetry

- **IoT Integration Platforms:** Use IoT integration platforms to streamline the flow of telemetry data into your BI system, enabling real-time monitoring and maintenance predictions.
- **Normalization:** Normalize telemetry data to fit BI tool requirements, ensuring consistent and accurate performance metrics analysis.

➢ Quality Control Systems

- **Automated Alerts:** Set up automated alerts within your BI solution based on real-time quality control data, enabling immediate corrective actions.
- **Integration with Manufacturing Execution Systems (MES):** Integrate quality control data with MES to provide a comprehensive view of production quality in real time.

➢ Employee Performance Monitors

- **HR Analytics Platforms:** Integrate employee performance data with HR analytics platforms within your BI solution to track productivity and operational efficiency.

- **Data Privacy Measures:** Implement strict data privacy measures to protect employee information while integrating it for performance analytics.

➢ Market Data Services

- **Data Subscription Services:** Subscribe to market data services that offer API access for real-time integration into your BI tools.
- **Customizable Feeds:** Customize data feeds to select only the most relevant market information for your business, reducing noise and focusing on actionable insights.

Δ Summary

Streamlining data integration across diverse data sources into a real-time BI solution enhances your ability to make informed decisions swiftly. By automating data flows, standardizing formats, and employing modern technologies like APIs, cloud platforms, and IoT integration tools, businesses can build a robust, real-time BI infrastructure that drives competitive advantage and operational efficiency.

Chapter-4

STEP 2 - Real-Time Analytics and Visualization

Continuing our exploration into building a real-time business intelligence solution, the next step is the implementation of real-time analytics and creating intuitive visualizations. This step is about equipping your business with the analytical prowess to navigate the vast data landscape effectively.

Here, let me introduce the DPAP framework to help you leverage the best of legacy BI and DW and the modern AI world.

The DPAP framework epitomizes the seamless fusion of technology and business intelligence in the purview of real-time analytics. At its foundation lies a robust Data Layer, tasked with the aggregation of heterogeneous data from CRM, ERP, and IoT platforms. Ascending from this base, the Processing Layer acts as the crucible for real-time data processing, supported by a flexible and agile Data Lake.

Points to Remember

- The foundation of effective real-time BI is identifying and harnessing key data sources–machinery sensors, supply chain data, and customer feedback.
- Automation and standardization are key to efficient data integration.
- Privacy and data management policies must be in place to protect sensitive information.
- Customizable and scalable integration approaches allow for flexibility as business needs evolve.
- IoT devices bring a new dimension to data collection, offering unparalleled insights but requiring careful attention to security and privacy.

"Let's dive into the Second step of the playbook "Real Time Analytics and Visualization", it's time to focus on interpreting this data to make instantaneous decisions."

With a streamlined data integration framework in place, the foundation for a powerful real-time BI solution is set, ready to transform data into actionable intelligence. We look towards the horizon where the power of real-time analysis awaits, ready to transform raw data into faster actionable insights and smarter strategic decisions.

The intelligent AI Layer applies machine learning, LLM, and generative and modern algorithms to distill this torrent of information into actionable insights.

These insights ascend to the Presentation Layer, where they are transformed into intuitive visualizations and prompt alerts, making the analysis accessible and actionable. Surrounding this structural hierarchy is a Feedback Loop, a sentinel of continuous improvement, ensuring that each layer's output informs and refines its predecessors, embodying a dynamic, self-optimizing cycle that is at the heart of the DPAP framework.

The DPAP framework uses the flow of data from collection to presentation, enhanced by AI and governed by a feedback loop for continuous improvement. Here is how it works :

- **Data Layer:** Collects information from various sources such as CRM, ERP, and IoT devices.
- **Processing Layer:** Involves real-time data processing and the consolidation of data into a data lake.
- **AI Layer:** Uses artificial intelligence to provide real-time analytics.
- **Presentation Layer:** Displays the processed data through visualization, reports, dashboards, and alerts.

- **Feedback Loop:** Indicates the process is cyclical, with the presentation layer feeding back to influence the data layer.

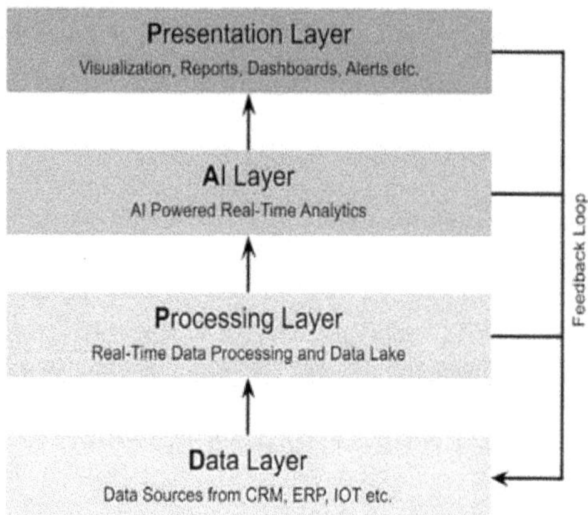

Δ Implementing Real-Time Analytics

The journey to mastering the landscape of data analytics begins with choosing the right tools for the task at hand.

- Choosing the Right Analytics Platforms

  The choice of an analytics platform is pivotal—similar to selecting the most reliable navigation system for a journey through diverse terrains. It's about finding a platform that not only fits your current needs but can scale and adapt as your business evolves. Selecting a particular data analytics and visualization tool is beyond the scope of this book. However, here are the steps to identify and select the best tool.

10 Steps to Select the Right Data Visualization Tool for Analytics:

1. **Clarify Visualization Goals:** Identify the specific types of visualizations you need for your analytics—charts, graphs, real-time dashboards, etc. Your goals might range from tracking production metrics in real time to visualizing customer behavior patterns.
2. **Assess Data Complexity:** Consider the complexity of the data you'll be visualizing. Ensure the tool can handle intricate data structures and large datasets efficiently, enabling clear and insightful visual representations.
3. **Determine Real-Time Capabilities:** Since real-time analytics is the focus, verify that the visualization tool can update visualizations instantaneously as new data comes in. This is crucial for operational monitoring and timely decision-making.
4. **Evaluate Customization Options:** The ability to customize visualizations is key. The tool should offer extensive customization options to tailor dashboards and charts to your specific needs, including branding and interactive elements.
5. **Check for Interactivity Features:** Interactive visualizations allow users to drill down into data for more detailed analysis. Look for tools that provide

interactive capabilities, such as tooltips, zoom, and dynamic filtering.

6. **Consider the Learning Curve:** Select a tool that balances advanced capabilities with usability. It should be accessible to users with varying levels of expertise in data analysis and visualization.
7. **Review Collaboration and Sharing Functions:** For teams, the ability to share visualizations and collaborate on dashboards is essential. Ensure the tool supports easy sharing, both internally and externally, with appropriate access controls.
8. **Investigate Mobile Accessibility:** In today's mobile-first world, check whether the visualization tool offers mobile access to dashboards and reports, allowing decision-makers to stay informed on the go.
9. **Understand the Support and Community:** Look into the support services provided, including training resources, customer service, and the presence of an active user community for advice and best practices.
10. **Trial and Feedback:** Utilize trial versions of the tools to create test visualizations with your data. Gather feedback from potential users to gauge the tool's effectiveness in meeting your visualization needs.

- Developing Custom Analytics Solutions

Data Visualization tools are very advanced in this modern ERA but you may have specific business needs to have a custom analytics solution. This is where developing custom analytics solutions comes into play, acting as your personalized GPS, meticulously designed to navigate your business's unique challenges and opportunities.

Custom analytics solutions are tailored to fit the specific contours of your business, allowing for a deeper and more precise understanding of your operational environment. These bespoke solutions can integrate disparate data sources, apply advanced analytics to your unique datasets, and present insights in a way that directly aligns with your strategic objectives.

Key Metrics for Manufacturing Success with Custom Analytics Solution

In the context of manufacturing, the journey towards operational excellence and strategic success is marked by several key metrics. Identifying and tracking these metrics is crucial as they serve as signposts, guiding your business towards its goals. Custom analytics solutions enable you to focus on these critical indicators by providing real-time visibility and actionable insights.

- **Production Efficiency:** Custom solutions can monitor production lines in real time, identifying bottlenecks and inefficiencies. By analyzing data from various stages of the manufacturing process, these tools can suggest optimizations for improving throughput and reducing waste.
- **Quality Control:** Leveraging data from quality inspections, machine sensors, and customer feedback, custom analytics can help maintain high product standards. Predictive models can forecast potential quality issues before they occur, allowing for preemptive action.
- **Inventory Management:** Advanced analytics tailored to your supply chain can optimize inventory levels, reducing holding costs and minimizing stockouts. By analyzing patterns in order fulfillment, material usage, and supplier performance, custom solutions ensure inventory is a strategic asset rather than a liability.
- **Equipment Maintenance:** Custom solutions can implement predictive maintenance strategies by analyzing telemetry data from machinery. This approach minimizes downtime and extends the life of equipment by scheduling maintenance based on actual usage and wear indicators.

- **Customer Satisfaction:** By integrating data from sales, customer service, and CRM systems, custom analytics solutions can provide deep insights into customer behavior and satisfaction. This enables the manufacturing firm to tailor products, services, and interactions to meet customer needs more effectively.

Developing custom analytics solutions requires a deep understanding of your business's data landscape and strategic goals. It involves selecting the right technologies, developing models that reflect your operational realities, and creating visualization tools that present insights in an intuitive and actionable manner. The investment in custom solutions pays dividends by providing a competitive edge, enhancing decision-making, and driving business success in ways that off-the-shelf solutions cannot match. But it's not for everyone.

Δ Effective Data Visualization Techniques

With a robust analytics framework in place, the next crucial step is to transform the raw data into compelling visual narratives. Effective data visualization not only simplifies complex datasets but also unveils the stories hidden within the numbers, making insights accessible and actionable across all levels of your organization.

- Business Monitoring Dashboards

  Imagine stepping into a command center, where screens and displays pulse with the heartbeat of your business operations. Dashboards are the most essential tool in this situation, offering a comprehensive, real-time view of your operational health. They aggregate data from various sources into a cohesive, interactive interface, enabling decision-makers to monitor performance metrics, track KPIs, and identify trends at a glance. These dashboards can be tailored to highlight the most relevant information, ensuring that operational oversight is both thorough and efficient.

- **Customization and Flexibility:** Tailor dashboards to display metrics that matter most to your business, from production volumes and inventory levels to sales figures and customer feedback.
- **Real-Time Updates:** Equip dashboards with the capability to refresh data in real-time, providing an up-to-the-minute overview of business operations.
- **Interactive Elements:** Incorporate interactive elements such as drill-downs and filters, allowing users to explore the data behind the visuals deeply.
- **Alerts and Notifications:** Set up alerts for critical thresholds or anomalies, ensuring that you can respond quickly to potential issues.

- **Integration with Other Systems:** Ensure dashboards can seamlessly integrate with other business systems, facilitating a unified view of your operations. This can help create prescriptive actions to be fed back into source systems for corrective and prohibitive actions.

➢ Mobile Apps for On-the-Go Monitoring

In today's fast-paced business environment, mobility and use of smart mobile devices is key. Data visualization mobile apps empower you with the flexibility to stay informed and make decisions, regardless of your location. These apps bring the power of your control room directly to your smartphone or tablet, offering tailored dashboards, alerts, and reporting tools designed for optimal viewing and interaction on smaller screens.

- **Accessibility:** Access crucial business metrics and reports anytime, anywhere, keeping your finger on the pulse of your operations.
- **Push Notifications:** Receive timely notifications about critical updates or changes, ensuring you're always in the loop.
- **User-Friendly Interface:** Benefit from interfaces designed for touch interaction, making it easy to navigate through complex data on the go.

- **Security:** Employ robust security measures to protect sensitive data accessed through mobile applications.
- **Offline Access:** Utilize features that allow data to be viewed even when an internet connection is unavailable, ensuring you're never without the insights you need.

➢ Engaging Stakeholders with Data

Clear and intuitive data visualizations bridge the gap between complex datasets and strategic decision-making. By democratizing data access, every stakeholder, from floor managers to the CEO, gains the ability to understand the business's current state and future trajectory. Visualizations enable a shared understanding, fostering a data-driven culture that aligns efforts towards common goals.

- **Tailored Views:** Provide stakeholders with customized views relevant to their roles and responsibilities, enhancing relevance and engagement.
- **Collaborative Tools:** Incorporate tools for sharing and discussing visualizations, encouraging collaboration and collective problem-solving.
- **Storytelling with Data:** Use visualizations to tell compelling stories about your business's challenges

and achievements, making data-driven insights memorable.

- **Training and Support:** Offer training sessions and resources to help stakeholders understand and utilize visualization tools effectively.
- **Feedback Loop:** Establish a feedback loop to continually refine and improve visualizations based on user experience and needs.

By focusing on these effective data visualization techniques, your business can enhance operational oversight, ensure mobility in monitoring, and engage stakeholders in meaningful ways, driving forward with clarity and confidence.

Δ Actionable Insights from Analytics

As we journey deeper into the realm of real-time business intelligence, we arrive at a critical juncture: transforming the vast sea of streaming data into a compass that guides us toward operational excellence and strategic victories.

➢ Translating Data into Operational Strategies

Navigating the complexities of the business landscape requires more than just data; it demands a blueprint that outlines the path to success. In this step, we focus on converting your data into actionable strategies that address your business's unique challenges and objectives. It's about curating insights from your analytics and mapping out a course of action that steers your operations toward efficiency, innovation, and competitiveness.

- **Strategic Alignment:** Ensure that the insights you curate align with your overarching business goals, creating a coherent strategy that moves all parts of the organization in the same direction.
- **Scenario Planning:** Use data to forecast various What-If scenarios and prepare strategies that account for different possible futures, enhancing your business's agility and resilience.
- **Customization and Personalization:** Tailor strategies to the specific needs of different departments or business units, recognizing that a one-size-fits-all approach may not be effective.
- **Continuous Optimization:** Treat your operational strategy as a living document, regularly revisiting and refining it based on new data and insights.
- **Stakeholder Engagement:** Involve key stakeholders in the strategy development process, ensuring buy-in and facilitating smoother implementation.

➢ Predictive Maintenance and Quality Control

Anticipating and preempting operational issues is similar to navigating through treacherous waters with a reliable forecast. Predictive analytics serves as your lighthouse, shining a light on potential hazards before they can impact your voyage. By applying predictive models to maintenance and quality control, you can significantly reduce downtime, prevent costly repairs, and ensure that your products consistently meet high standards of quality.

- **Proactive Measures:** Implement predictive maintenance schedules that preempt equipment failures, keeping your operations running smoothly without unexpected interruptions.
- **Quality Assurance:** Leverage analytics to identify patterns or anomalies that could indicate quality issues, allowing for adjustments before they affect the end product.
- **Cost Reduction:** By avoiding unplanned maintenance and ensuring product quality, predictive analytics can lead to substantial cost savings and efficiency gains.
- **Risk Management:** Minimize the risk of operational disruptions and reputational damage by maintaining high standards of reliability and quality.

- **Enhanced Decision-Making:** Empower managers and operators with data-driven insights that support informed decisions about maintenance and quality control.

Δ Real-life Example of Analytics-driven Turnaround

To illuminate the power of actionable insights from analytics, let us share the story of a company (we worked with) on the brink of operational chaos. Through the strategic application of analytics, this business not only averted potential disaster but also charted a new course toward unprecedented growth and profitability. Their journey from data to strategy, through the implementation of real-time analytics and a renewed focus on quality control, serves as a beacon for others navigating the complexity of modern business.

It saved this company not only on recalls but also better quality control to gain customer trust and thereby increase profits.

Δ Summary

In this chapter, we've equipped you with the necessary tools and insights to chart a successful course through the data-driven landscape of the manufacturing industry.

STEP 2: Real-Time Analytics and Visualization

We also strategized on how to harness analytics for crafting operational strategies, implementing predictive maintenance, and ensuring quality control—turning data into a navigational tool that guides your business toward success. These actionable insights are the treasure map leading to operational efficiencies, reduced costs, and a competitive edge in the marketplace.

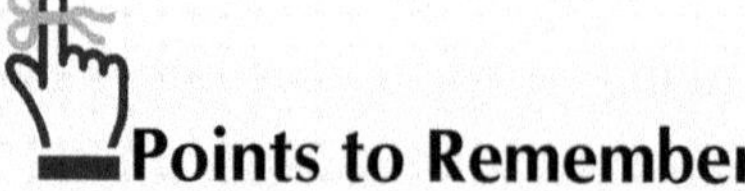

Points to Remember

- The right analytics platform acts as your guide through the data-driven journey of your business.
- Custom Tailored analytics solutions help address your business's unique challenges.
- Dashboards and mobile apps are your eyes and ears, keeping you connected to the pulse of your operations.
- Analytics-derived strategies provide the direction needed to navigate your business effectively.
- Predictive analytics act as your early warning system, helping you anticipate and navigate around potential issues.

What's next

"Shifting our focus from the development of strategies informed by our analytics, we move to the next essential, third step of our playbook–Automating Decision Processes."

This pivotal shift in our journey from 'what' within our data to executing the 'how,' enables us to deploy our insights rapidly and efficiently. Automating these processes empowers us to respond in real time to the dynamic demands of the business environment.

Let's read further.

Chapter-5

STEP 3 - Automating Decision Processes

In the vast narrative of modern business, there's a recurring villain named Delay. This Devil is infamous for causing a cascade of inventory waste, a direct consequence of manual decision-making. It's a chilling fact that in the time it takes for a human to make a single decision, a well-tuned machine could have made thousands.

Automation can be achieved in a very simple 6-step process. The two building blocks of this diagram will be discussed in depth in this chapter.

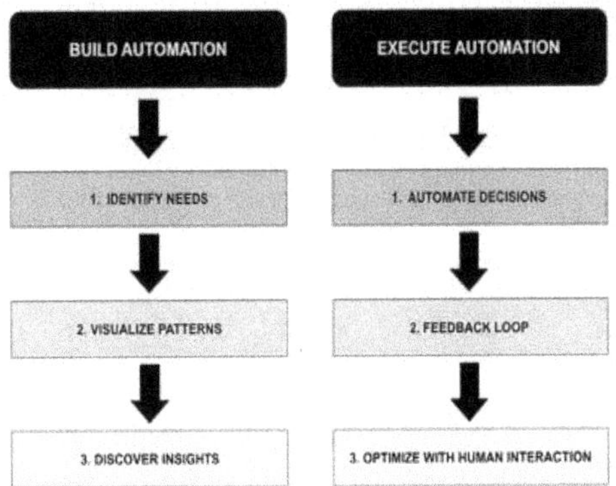

1. Building Automation into BI

In our narrative where time is the currency of success, we introduce Automation as the innovative machinery that revolutionizes the assembly line of decision-making within Business Intelligence (BI).

- Software Solutions for Decision Automation

  Our toolbox can be equipped with a spectrum of software solutions, each precision-engineered to automate elements of the decision-making process. These tools are the diligent robots on the factory floor of our data operation, assuming control of the repetitive tasks and freeing our human strategists to focus on breakthrough thinking and innovation. While providing the names of the specific tools is beyond the scope of this book, reviewing current cloud leaders and the toolkit they have to offer would guide in selecting and hand-picking the right toolset.

- AI and Machine Learning Models for BI

  In the high-tech foundry of modern business, Artificial Intelligence (AI) and Machine Learning (ML) models stand as the pinnacle of innovation, akin to robotic maestros in a symphony of data. These advanced systems do not just process information; they distill it into strategic foresight, operating with precision and endurance that human analysis cannot hope to match. As they assimilate data, they uncover patterns, akin to an experienced quality inspector who spots defects before they become systemic issues.

Take, for instance, a global manufacturing giant like Toyota. They employ AI to predict which parts in their vehicles might fail and when. By analyzing warranty data and customer feedback with ML algorithms, Toyota can proactively address issues before they escalate, saving on costly recalls and maintaining its reputation for quality.

In retail, Amazon's ML algorithms are a game-changer. They analyze consumer behavior, seasonal trends, and purchase histories, enabling stock optimization at warehouses and ensuring that the 'right product reaches the right customer at the right time', a testament to their customer-centric approach that has made Amazon a household name.

From Bottlenecks to Breakthroughs: Drive Measurable Growth with Strategic Supply Chain Optimization

Δ Introduction

In the competitive world of audio device manufacturing, staying ahead requires not just innovation in product development but also in navigating the complex global supply chain. A mid-sized company, with revenues ranging from $50 million to $500 million, faced significant challenges in understanding and optimizing its supply chain due to factors like seasonality, competitive pressures, and global logistics challenges exacerbated by geopolitical tensions.

Δ Challenges

The company encountered several obstacles that hindered its ability to maintain smooth operations and reduce costs:

- **Global Supply Chain Complexity:** Difficulty in mapping and understanding the intricate global supply network.
- **Seasonality and Demand Forecasting:** Struggles with predicting demand fluctuations due to seasonal trends.
- **Logistics Challenges:** Disruptions due to geopolitical tensions, leading to delays and increased costs.

- **Limited IT Resources:** A constrained IT budget and workforce made it challenging to implement necessary technological solutions.

Δ Solution

To address these challenges, the company embarked on a strategic supply chain optimization initiative, leveraging the latest in technology and data analytics. The solution comprised several key components:

- **Cloud Solutions and Data Warehousing:** Adopting cloud-based solutions facilitated scalable and flexible data storage and processing capabilities. Following Ralph Kimball's best practices, the company implemented a dimensional model for the data warehouse, enabling efficient data organization and retrieval.
- **Business Intelligence Tools:** Real-time BI tools were deployed to analyze data across the supply chain. These tools provided insights into bottlenecks, predicted shortages or delays, and suggested alternative suppliers or routes.
- **Security and Governance:** With the introduction of new technologies, ensuring data security and governance became paramount. The company implemented robust security measures and

governance frameworks to protect sensitive information.

- **Advanced Analytics and Machine Learning:** Utilizing generative AI, RAG models, and machine learning, the company could predict demand more accurately, identify potential supply chain disruptions before they occurred, and optimize inventory levels.
- **Predictive and Prescriptive Analytics:** These technologies allowed the company to not just predict future trends but also prescribe actionable strategies to mitigate risks and capitalize on opportunities.

Δ Benefits

The strategic supply chain optimization initiative brought about significant benefits:

- **Enhanced Operational Efficiency:** By identifying and addressing bottlenecks in real time, the company could streamline operations, reducing delays and costs.
- **Improved Demand Forecasting:** Advanced analytics enabled more accurate prediction of demand, allowing for better inventory management and reduced stockouts or overstock situations.

- **Cost Reduction:** Optimizing the supply chain led to significant cost savings, from reduced inventory holding costs to minimized logistics expenses, directly impacting the bottom line positively

Δ Summary

For the mid-sized audio device manufacturer, transitioning from supply chain bottlenecks to breakthroughs was not just about adopting new technologies but about strategically leveraging real-time business intelligence, advanced analytics, and data warehousing to drive measurable growth. This initiative not only addressed the immediate challenges of global supply chain complexity, demand forecasting, and logistics disruptions but also set the foundation for sustained operational efficiency and profitability. By prioritizing solutions that offered quantifiable benefits, the company could improve its competitive advantage in the dynamic global market, demonstrating the power of strategic supply chain optimization in achieving business objectives.

In every sector, from automotive to entertainment to retail, AI and ML are transforming the landscape. With every byte of data they process, they are writing the future of business—a future where data-driven decisions are not just smart but are imbued with the power to propel businesses to new heights of success.

In the context of real-time BI for manufacturing, specific AI and ML models stand out for their ability to streamline processes and enhance decision-making:

- **Predictive Analytics Models:** Utilized for forecasting machine maintenance needs and production demands to minimize downtime and optimize production schedules.
- **Classification Models:** Applied to categorize product defects or classify production batches for quality assurance and control.
- **Clustering Models:** Employed to optimize supply chain logistics by grouping similar demand patterns or production characteristics.
- **Anomaly Detection Models:** Integral for identifying irregularities in real-time sensor data that could indicate equipment malfunctions or safety hazards.
- **Neural Networks:** Particularly useful for complex tasks like visual quality inspections where pattern recognition is key for identifying defects.

- **Time Series Forecasting:** Essential for tracking and predicting inventory levels over time to ensure material availability aligns with production needs.
- **Decision Trees and Random Forests:** Deployed for assessing the likelihood of production issues based on a range of input variables, from equipment performance metrics to environmental conditions.

  These models transform real-time data streams into actionable intelligence, giving you the tools to anticipate, plan, and act swiftly to maintain seamless operations.

Δ *Balancing Automation with Human Oversight*

Yet, as any seasoned CIO knows, the smartest production line blends the precision of automation with the irreplaceable value of human expertise. It is the human touch that fine-tunes the machinery, that troubleshoots the unforeseen, ensuring that our automated BI systems operate within the nuanced realities of the business world.

Through the strategic deployment of automation in BI with Machine Learning models, we are not just speeding up processes; we are redefining the manufacturing blueprint of business operations, where data-driven decisions are produced with the speed, accuracy, and quality that only a well-oiled machine can deliver.

2. Streamlining Operations with Automation

Automation, our hero, to fight with the Devil of "Delay", embarks on a noble quest to conquer inefficiency and elevate the levels of consistency and precision.

➢ Optimizing Supply Chain Decisions

Thanks to automation, supply chain operations have become faster and more dependable. enabling the alignment of the inventory perfectly with customer demand, ensuring just the right amount of stock at all times. The process of moving products from the manufacturer to the customer would be seamless, operating like a well-directed stream, efficient and error-free. This will not only save time but also significantly reduce the chances of overstocking or running out of products.

Optimize, Not Compromise: Tailored Inventory Management for Peak Performance

Δ Introduction

In those competitive landscape of medical device manufacturing, managing inventory efficiently is paramount. A mid-sized company, generating $50 million to $500 million in revenue, faced significant challenges with inventory backlogs and replenishment. Their unique business model, supplying devices on consignment to hospitals and doctors, compounded these challenges, as inventory was only consumed in response to patient injuries, with reimbursement tied to insurance claims and HCPCS codes.

Δ Challenges

The company encountered several critical issues impacting its operational efficiency and profitability:

- **Inventory Backlogs:** Excessive stock levels leading to increased storage costs and capital tied up in unsold inventory.
- **Inefficient Replenishment:** Difficulty in predicting and managing inventory levels to meet fluctuating demand.

- **Complex Claims Processing:** The need for accurate diagnostic codes and claim filings for insurance reimbursements added layers of complexity.
- **Stale Inventory Costs:** Losses incurred from inventory that remained unused or became obsolete over time.

Δ Solution

To address these challenges, the company embarked on a comprehensive strategy leveraging the latest in technology and data analytics:

- **Cloud Solutions and Data Warehousing:** Implementing cloud-based storage and processing solutions, the company adopted a dimensional data model as recommended by data warehousing expert Ralph Kimball. This approach facilitated efficient data organization and retrieval, crucial for real-time inventory management.
- **Business Intelligence (BI) Tools:** Real-time BI tools were deployed to analyze data across all providers, warehouse locations, doctors, and claims. This enabled the identification of bottlenecks, prediction of inventory overages or shortages, and optimization of inventory replenishment strategies.

- **Advanced Analytics and Machine Learning:** The use of generative AI, RAG models, predictive and prescriptive analytics, and machine learning technologies allowed for more accurate demand forecasting and inventory management, reducing the risk of overstocking or stockouts.
- **Security and Governance:** With the introduction of advanced technologies, ensuring the security and governance of data became a priority. The company implemented robust security measures and governance frameworks to protect sensitive information and comply with healthcare regulations.

Δ Benefits

The strategic overhaul of the inventory management system yielded significant benefits:

- **Reduced Inventory Costs:** Optimized inventory levels led to lower storage costs and minimized capital tied up in unsold stock.
- **Improved Operational Efficiency:** Enhanced demand forecasting and replenishment strategies ensured that inventory levels were aligned with actual consumption patterns, reducing waste and improving service levels.
- **Streamlined Claims Processing:** The integration of BI tools with claims processing systems facilitated

faster and more accurate filing, improving cash flow and reducing administrative burdens.

Δ Summary

For the mid-sized medical device manufacturer, transitioning to a data-driven inventory management system was a game-changer. By leveraging cloud solutions, real-time business intelligence, and advanced analytics, the company not only overcame its inventory management challenges but also set a new standard for operational efficiency in the industry. This strategic initiative not only reduced costs and waste but also enhanced the company's ability to serve its clients promptly and accurately, ultimately leading to improved profitability and competitive advantage.

Δ *Reducing Downtime Through Predictive Maintenance*

With the sixth sense of predictive maintenance, it's like having a crystal ball for factory machines. It uses sensors and AI to catch problems with gears and parts before they break down. Instead of waiting for something to go wrong and then fixing it, this smart system spots issues early, making sure machines keep running smoothly. Think of it as a superhero for the manufacturing world, using its powers to keep everything running without hiccups, making factories more efficient and cutting down on unexpected repair time.

Δ *Smart Demand-Driven Production Scheduling*

In a dynamic quest for efficiency, mid-sized manufacturing companies can tremendously save production costs by utilizing a demand-driven production model, leveraging real-time Business Intelligence (BI) and advanced analytics. Companies that have seasonality would benefit by utilizing this model. Here is a case that talks about this transformation for the travel accessories producer.

This transformative journey navigates through the challenges of fluctuating market demands, aiming to optimize production schedules and cut costs without compromising quality. Through strategic technological integration and data-driven decision-making, the company achieves operational excellence, setting a new standard for sustainability and competitiveness in the global market.

Cut Costs, Not Corners, Smart Scheduling for Demand-Driven Production using Real-Time BI

Δ Introduction

In the dynamic world of travel accessories and outdoor gear, a mid-sized global manufacturing company faced significant challenges in aligning production schedules with fluctuating regional demands. With revenues ranging from $10 million to $500 million, the company sought to optimize its production processes without overproducing or unnecessarily relocating inventory, aiming for a demand-driven production model that could cut costs without compromising quality.

Δ Challenges

The journey to efficient production scheduling was hindered by several key issues:

- **Inconsistent Demand Forecasting:** Difficulty in accurately predicting regional demand led to overproduction or shortages.
- **Inefficient Production Scheduling:** Existing schedules were not aligned with real-time demand, causing inventory imbalances.

- **High Inventory Relocation Costs:** Excess production in one region necessitated costly inventory transfers to meet demand in another.

Δ Solution

To address these challenges, the company embarked on a strategic overhaul of its production scheduling processes, leveraging the latest in technology and analytics:

- **Cloud Solutions and Data Warehousing:** By adopting cloud-based solutions and implementing a dimensional data model as per Ralph Kimball's recommendations, the company ensured a scalable, efficient foundation for data management. This setup allowed for the integration of data from various global production houses and regional sales data.
- **Real-Time Business Intelligence (BI) Tools:** The deployment of real-time BI tools enabled the company to analyze data across all regions, identifying demand patterns and adjusting production schedules accordingly. This approach allowed for dynamic scheduling, balancing workloads across machines and shifts in response to changing demands.
- **Advanced Analytics and Machine Learning:** Utilizing generative AI, RAG models, and predictive and prescriptive analytics, the company could

forecast demand more accurately and optimize production schedules. This technology also facilitated the identification of potential bottlenecks and provided recommendations for process improvements.

∆ Benefits

The implementation of these solutions brought about significant improvements:

- **Reduced Inventory Costs:** By aligning production with actual demand, the company minimized overproduction and reduced the need for inventory relocation, leading to significant cost savings.
- **Increased Operational Efficiency:** Real-time scheduling and demand forecasting streamlined production processes, enhancing overall efficiency.
- **Improved Profit Margins:** Lower inventory costs and increased efficiency directly contributed to improved profitability, allowing the company to invest further in innovation and market expansion.

Δ Summary

For the mid-sized manufacturer in the travel accessories and outdoor industry, adopting a smart, demand-driven production scheduling approach using real-time BI and advanced analytics marked a turning point. This strategic move not only addressed the immediate challenges of overproduction and high inventory costs but also set the stage for sustainable growth and competitiveness. By cutting costs without cutting corners, the company demonstrated that with the right technology and approach, it's possible to achieve operational excellence and meet the ever-changing demands of the global market.

3. Top 5 Challenges and Solutions in Automation

➢ Integration Complexity

- **Challenge:** Integrating automation technologies into existing systems can be complex, especially in environments with outdated infrastructure or diverse platforms.
- **Solution:** Employ middleware solutions, AI, Generative AI and RPA tools and APIs that act as bridges between different systems, facilitating smoother integration. Consider consulting with integration specialists to devise a strategy that minimizes disruption.

➢ Skill Gaps and Training

- **Challenge:** The shift towards automation requires a workforce skilled in new technologies, yet many organizations face skill gaps.
- **Solution:** Invest in comprehensive training programs and partnerships with educational institutions to upskill employees. Additionally, adopting user-friendly automation tools with extensive support and documentation can ease the transition.

➢ Data Privacy and Security

- **Challenge:** Automation often involves processing vast amounts of sensitive data, raising concerns about privacy and security.
- **Solution:** Implement robust data encryption, access controls, and regular security audits and compliance practices as per your industry segment to protect sensitive information and keep it under compliance. Staying updated with compliance regulations and best practices in cybersecurity can also mitigate risks.

➢ High Initial Costs

- **Challenge:** The initial investment in automation technology can be significant, deterring some organizations from adopting it.
- **Solution:** Conduct a thorough cost-benefit analysis to understand the long-term savings and efficiency gains. Exploring options like automation as a service (AaaS) can also reduce upfront costs by offering a subscription-based model.

➢ Resistance to Change

- **Challenge:** Employees may resist automation due to fears of job displacement or distrust of new systems.

- **Solution:** Engage employees early in the automation process, highlighting the benefits such as reduced manual labor and opportunities for higher-value work. Transparent communication and involving employees in decision-making can foster a positive outlook towards change.

Δ Summary

As we turn the page on the "Automating Decision Process" step of our playbook, we learnt how to implement Automation—a hero in the manufacturing narrative, transforming age-old decision-making into a model of modern efficiency. We've seen how this champion of efficiency conquers the villainous Delay, turning faster insights into smarter actions with the help of advanced software, AI, and a balance of human intuition.

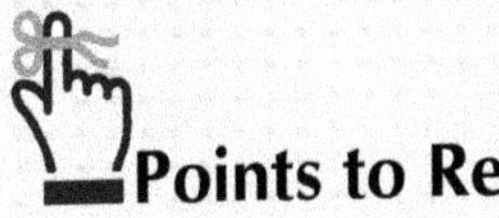

Points to Remember

- Decision Automation is the hero to eliminate the waste brought by Delay.
- AI and Machine Learning are like the smartest computer programs, predicting problems before they happen and finding the best solutions super-fast.
- The real magic happens when people and these smart systems work together.
- The key point to remember – is that the right tools and strategies can lead to a future of efficiency and success.

When the collective moves in the same direction, success naturally follows.

In the Fourth step of our playbook, we'll shift gears to "Strategy Execution in Real-Time," where we will ensure that our manufacturing operations don't just run, but sprint towards success with precision and adaptability.

Chapter-6

Step 4 - Strategy Execution in Real-Time

In the world of manufacturing, the ability to execute strategy in real time is similar to navigating through a busy factory floor with precision and purpose. This chapter draws upon the lessons learned from the first three steps of our playbook—Building Automation into BI, Streamlining Operations with Automation, and Overcoming Automation Challenges—to lay out the roadmap for implementing strategies that respond dynamically to the pulse of the market.

This chapter is all about the execution of these strategies and the concise steps given here would help you to follow and adopt RealTime Business Intelligence in an easy and precise manner.

Step 4 - Strategy Execution in Real-Time

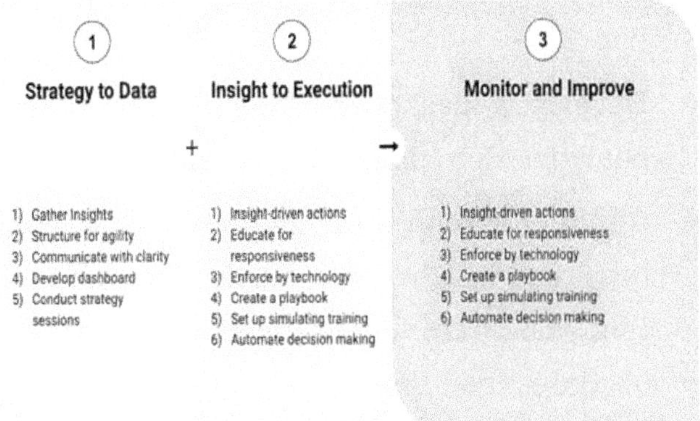

1. Synchronizing Strategy with RealTime Data:

➢ The Convergence of Data and Action

In order to see the fruition of strategy and converge into action, please follow this 5-step process:

- **Gather your insights:** Pull data from AI-driven predictive maintenance reports and real-time quality control assessments.
- **Structure for agility:** Design organizational workflows that can shift gears at a moment's notice, much like adjusting production lines for a sudden change in product demand.
- **Communicate with clarity:** Establish communication channels that deliver actionable data to the right teams without delay—clear and

direct like the signals on a factory floor. Action Points

- **Develop a dashboard:** that integrates real-time analytics for a comprehensive view.
- **Conduct regular strategy sessions:** to align real-time data insights with current production goals. Implement a cross-departmental response protocol to address real-time data findings.

2. From Insights to Execution:

➢ The Blueprint for Action

- **Standardizing insight-driven actions:** Integrate insights into the standard operating procedures of the manufacturing process, so responses become automatic and efficient.
- **Educating for responsiveness:** Just as a machine operator is trained to respond to the control panel's prompts, train your teams to act swiftly and knowledgeably based on data cues.
- **Technological enforcement:** Equip your factory with the latest in smart manufacturing technology that reinforces best practices and supports top-tier operational performance.

- Execution Tactics
  - Create a playbook for different scenarios based on data trends to guide immediate actions.
  - Set up training simulations using real-time data to enhance team responsiveness.
  - Upgrade machinery and systems to ensure they support automated decision-making.

3. Monitor Success of Real-Time Strategy Execution:

- The Metrics of Progress
  - Establish Key Performance Indicators (KPIs) that measure the effectiveness of real-time decision-making in the manufacturing process.
  - Develop feedback loops that allow for the continuous refinement of strategies based on real-world outcomes and data analysis.
  - Share stories of successful strategy implementations that highlight the positive impacts of real-time execution on ROI and operational efficiency.
- Evaluation Framework
  - Monitor KPIs such as production uptime, rate of return, and product quality for immediate insight into the success of executed strategies.

- Regularly review feedback from floor managers and operators to adjust strategies for greater efficiency.
- Document case studies of strategy successes and learnings, using them as a knowledge base for future strategy development.

Δ Summary

Our strategies are not just plans on paper; they are living, breathing actions that evolve at the pace of the market. Our success is measured through key performance indicators, ensuring our strategies not only respond to the current market but actively shape the manufacturing landscape of tomorrow. This is the blueprint for a future where real-time strategy execution drives industry leadership.

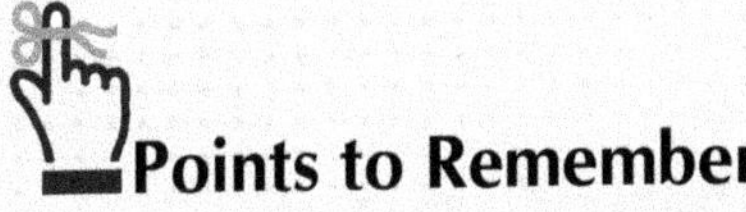

- Integration is Key: Seamless integration of real-time data with automated systems is crucial for timely and informed decision-making.
- Agility in Workflow: A nimble operational structure allows for quick pivoting in response to data insights, keeping production lines adaptable to change.
- Empowered Teams: Training and equipping teams with the right tools ensures that insights are promptly translated into action.
- Measure to Manage: Establishing KPIs is essential to measure the effectiveness of real-time strategy execution and to foster continuous improvement.
- Feedback Fuels Growth: Regular feedback loops are vital for refining strategies and maintaining the cycle of learning and evolving within the manufacturing process.

Without any data available, one is essentially sharing a personal opinion

With a strategy that turns insights into action, in the next and final step of our playbook "Creating a Data-Driven Culture", we'll ensure that your entire ecosystem is aligned to support these real-time decisions. Join us as we delve into the cultural shift that empowers every layer of an organization to embrace data, driving collective progress and shaping the future

Chapter-7

STEP 5 - Creating a Data-Driven Culture

Satya Nadella, CEO of Microsoft said in a 2016 earning call -"Data is the new electricity."

A data-driven culture is not just an operational adjustment; it's a transformation at the core of our business,". This insight sets the stage for our journey into fostering an environment where data is not just present but is the cornerstone of every decision, strategy, and innovation. In this narrative, we delve into the essence of building a culture that breathes data, transforming every challenge into an opportunity for growth.

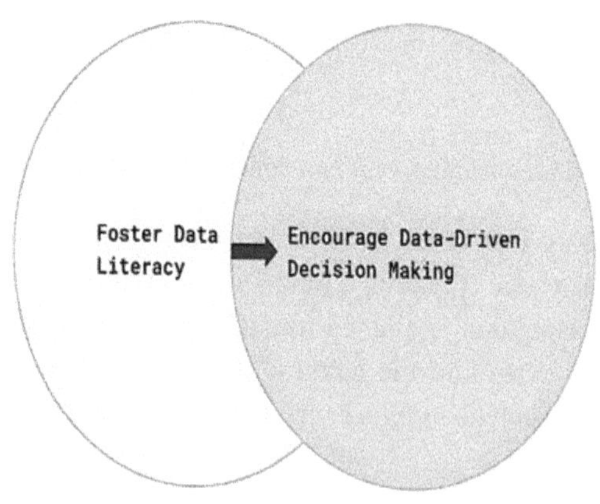

1. Fostering Data Literacy

To effectively engage with the volume and variety of data around us, it's essential for everyone to become proficient in its language.

In the digital age, your roadmap must include cultivating data literacy across all levels of the organization. Data literacy is as crucial as operational expertise, and it begins with comprehensive education.

Δ *Educational Programs and Workshops*

Implement structured learning programs tailored to different roles within the organization, focusing on the significance and application of data. Workshops should be practical and interactive, allowing team members to explore data's impact on business outcomes.

Δ *Creating Data Champions Within Teams*

Nominate individuals with a knack for data analysis to become Data Champions. These champions will spearhead data initiatives, mentor their colleagues, and foster an environment where data is an integral part of the decision-making fabric.

Δ *Resources and Tools for Self-Learning*

Develop an internal platform or resource center where team members can access data tools and learning materials at their own pace. This repository should be dynamic, and continuously updated with the latest in data analytics trends, tools, and best practices.

By embedding data literacy into the organization's DNA, you set the stage for a culture that not only understands data but also actively seeks it out to drive strategic decisions and innovation.

2. Encouraging Data-Driven Decision Making

"The heart of a data-driven culture is in making informed and data-driven decision making."

Creating a data-driven culture pivots on the decisions that are informed and substantiated by robust data analytics. For a CIO or technical leader, it's about making data the trusted advisor in every meeting room.

Δ *Incentives for Data-Based Decisions*

Establish a reward system for teams and individuals who successfully utilize data to drive business decisions. This could take the form of recognition programs, bonuses, or career advancement opportunities, which reinforces the value placed on data-centric thinking.

Δ *Showcasing Success Stories and Wins*

Regularly communicate instances where data-driven decision-making has resulted in significant business wins. Whether through internal newsletters, meetings, or dashboards, highlight these success stories to illustrate the tangible benefits of a data-oriented approach.

Δ *Overcoming Resistance to Data-Driven Changes*

Transitioning to a data-centric culture can meet with resistance. Counter this by providing clear examples and case studies that demonstrate the efficacy of data-driven decisions. Support this with continuous education and transparency to foster trust and buy-in from all organizational levels.

By actively promoting and facilitating a data-driven approach to decision-making, CIOs can engrain a mindset across the organization that not only values data but sees it as the key driver for innovation, efficiency, and competitive advantage. Here's a Use Case Scenario of how encouraging Data-Driven Decisions can enhance speed, agility & efficiency.

Lead with Speed: Fast-Track Decision-Making with Real-Time Business Intelligence

Δ Introduction

In the fast-paced world of electronic manufacturing, a mid-sized company with revenues between $100 million and $1 billion faced significant challenges. Despite dealing in both B2B and direct-to-consumer markets, their ability to make swift strategic decisions was hampered by slow BI and DW systems. The need for a solution that could provide real-time insights to the leadership team was critical to staying competitive and responsive in a market dominated by larger entities with more substantial marketing budgets.

Δ Challenges

The company encountered several obstacles in its quest for agility and market responsiveness:

- **Delayed Insights:** Existing BI and DW systems were slow, hindering timely decision-making.
- **Limited Market Outreach:** A constrained budget prevented extensive marketing efforts.
- **Competition with Larger Entities:** Struggling to compete against larger organizations with more resources.

- **Need for Real-Time Data:** A lack of immediate access to operational and external market data.

Δ Solution

To overcome these challenges, the company embarked on a comprehensive digital transformation:

- **Cloud Solutions and Data Warehousing:** By migrating to cloud-based solutions and adopting Ralph Kimball's dimensional modeling for data warehousing, the company ensured scalable, efficient data management. This foundation enabled the integration of diverse data sources, including real-time operational data and external factors like market trends and geopolitical events.
- **Advanced BI Tools:** The implementation of cutting-edge BI tools allowed for the real-time analysis of both internal operations and external market data. These tools provided the leadership team with actionable insights, enabling swift strategic decisions.
- **Predictive and Prescriptive Analytics:** Leveraging modern technologies such as generative AI, RAG models, and machine learning, the company could forecast future trends and receive recommendations for strategic actions. This approach not only anticipated market demands but also identified potential operational efficiencies.

- **Security and Governance:** With the introduction of advanced data solutions, the company prioritized security and governance to protect sensitive information and ensure compliance with industry regulations.

Δ Benefits

The strategic overhaul yielded significant advantages:

- **Enhanced Decision-Making Speed:** Real-time data access allowed the leadership team to make informed decisions swiftly, improving responsiveness to market changes.
- **Increased Competitive Edge:** The ability to quickly adjust strategies based on comprehensive market insights helped the company compete more effectively against larger rivals.
- **Cost Efficiency:** Optimized production and marketing strategies, informed by real-time data, led to better resource allocation and reduced waste, enhancing profitability.

∆ Summary

For the mid-sized electronic manufacturing company, the transition to a real-time BI-driven decision-making process marked a significant turning point. "Lead with Speed: Fast-Track Decision Making with Real-Time Business Intelligence" not only addressed the immediate challenges of slow data analysis and competitive pressures but also set the stage for sustainable growth and market agility. By leveraging cloud solutions, advanced analytics, and robust data governance, the company positioned itself to navigate the complexities of the electronic manufacturing industry with newfound speed and efficiency, proving that strategic agility and informed decision-making are within reach, even for mid-sized players in a competitive landscape.

3. Building a Supportive Infrastructure

"For a tree to bear fruit, it must be planted in fertile soil and must be provided the right environment to grow."

The success of a data-driven culture is largely contingent upon the infrastructure put in place. Just as a tree's growth is dependent on both the fertility of the soil and the nurturing it receives, so too does the data environment require a robust foundation and ongoing support.

Δ *Technological Infrastructure for Data Access*

It's imperative to equip each team member with the necessary tools and access to data, much like providing every craftsman in a workshop with quality instruments. This equal footing allows for a democratization of data, where insights and innovation can come from any level within the organization.

Δ *Policies and Frameworks to Support BI*

Develop and enforce policies and frameworks that serve to cultivate and maintain the data environment. These guidelines are the caretakers of data integrity and governance, ensuring that the data used to inform decisions is accurate, timely, and secure.

Δ *Leadership's Role in a Data-Driven Culture*

Leaders must embody the principles of a data-driven culture, making strategic decisions rooted in data, which serves as a powerful example for the rest of the organization. By visibly and consistently relying on data to guide actions, leadership reinforces the importance of a data-centric approach.

By creating a fertile ground with the right technological tools, governance structures, and leadership models, a data-driven culture can take root, flourish, and sustain the growth of a forward-thinking, data-savvy organization.

Δ **Summary**

In the realm of manufacturing, the integration of a data-driven culture is akin to mastering a complex production process. We've delved into the essentials of data literacy, proactive decision-making, and robust infrastructure, crafting a blueprint for a transformative journey. It's a journey marked by the evolution of operations, the elevation of strategy, and the empowerment of every team member through data.

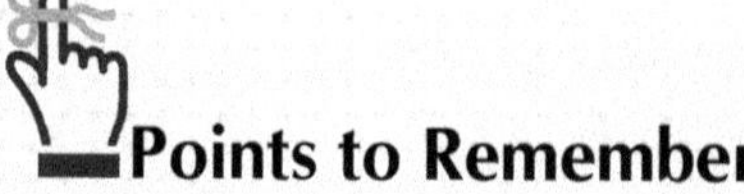

- Data literacy forms the bedrock of a culture where decisions are guided by insight rather than intuition.
- Advocating for data-driven decisions signals a pivotal shift in the organizational mindset, fostering a new era of analytical thinking.
- Narratives of success serve as powerful catalysts, inspiring teams to embrace the value of data in sculpting the future of manufacturing.
- A strong infrastructure lays the groundwork for seamless access to data, ensuring it is a shared and valuable resource across all levels of the company.
- Exemplary leadership in data utilization sets a precedent, establishing a standard for decision-making that resonates throughout the organization.

Having established a robust basis in Real-Time Business Intelligence, it's time to put our five-step strategy into action as we explore ways to keep the momentum going and continue to innovate.

As we turn the page on this chapter, we stand at the threshold of a new era. Armed with the knowledge and strategies to embed data into our culture, we're ready to sail into the future, continuously innovating and redefining what it means to be a truly data-driven organization.

Part III

BEYOND THE PLAYBOOK

Chapter-8

Scaling Your BI Initiatives

"Growth is not a matter of luck; it's created with the collaborative effort of different elements."

This is especially true in the context of Business Intelligence (BI) where scaling is both an art and a science. As your business grows, so does the complexity of your data and the need for sophisticated BI strategies. This chapter will guide you through expanding your BI capabilities without losing the nimbleness and insight that characterized your earlier successes.

1. Assessing Current BI Capabilities

Before we set sail on this voyage of expansion, we must understand the vessel we're in.

➢ Evaluation of Existing BI Infrastructure

- Review Current BI Systems: Start with a comprehensive audit of your existing Business Intelligence infrastructure, similar to conducting a narrative review of a story.

- **Identify Strengths:** Determine the strengths of your BI 'characters'—the tools, systems, and processes that are currently effective.
- **Spot Development Needs:** Identify the 'plot points' or areas within your BI strategy that require development or improvement to enhance the overall performance.

➢ Identifying Scalability Bottlenecks

- **Pinpoint Growth Hindrances:** Identify specific elements within your BI strategy that may impede scalability and growth.
- **Assess Technologies:** Evaluate if outdated technologies are part of the bottleneck, requiring updates or replacement.
- **Review Data Structures:** Examine your data structures for inflexibility that may hinder the ability to scale, indicating a need for restructuring to accommodate the expanding narrative of your business.

2. Strategies for Scaling BI:

Now, let's explore the paths of growth for your BI strategy.

➢ Incremental vs. Big Leap Approaches

When deciding how to upgrade your Business Intelligence (BI) system, you can choose between two main strategies

- The Incremental approach or
- The Big Leap approach.

The Incremental approach involves making small, manageable updates and improvements over time. This method is less risky and allows for steady progress without overwhelming your team or budget. It's like building a house brick by brick, ensuring each addition fits perfectly before moving on. However, this approach might be slower and could delay significant advancements.

The Big Leap approach is about making major changes all at once. It's riskier, as it involves investing a lot of resources upfront and can disrupt current operations, but it can also lead to rapid improvements and competitive advantages. Think of it as demolishing an old house to build a new one from scratch; it's a chance to quickly modernize but requires careful planning to avoid pitfalls.

Ultimately, the choice between Incremental and Big Leap approaches depends on your company's appetite for risk, resource availability, and how urgently you need to see changes in your BI capabilities.

➢ Cloud-based BI Solutions for Scalability

Cloud-based Business Intelligence (BI) solutions offer a flexible and scalable approach to managing your company's data and analytics needs. By using cloud technology, your BI system can easily adjust to your business's growing demands without the need for expensive hardware upgrades or extensive IT resources.

This is like renting a house that can magically expand or contract based on how much space you need, eliminating the hassle of moving or rebuilding. The cloud provides access to powerful computing resources and storage capacity on demand, meaning you can handle more data and run complex analyses without worrying about performance bottlenecks. Plus, with pay-as-you-go pricing models, you only pay for what you use, making it a cost-effective solution for businesses of all sizes. Whether your company is experiencing rapid growth, or you need to scale down operations temporarily, cloud-based BI solutions offer the agility to adapt quickly, ensuring your data strategy remains aligned with your business objectives.

3. Maintaining Quality, Compliance and Agility

As the narrative of your business unfolds, maintaining the integrity of the story is crucial.

- Managing Compliance for healthcare manufacturing

  In the world of healthcare manufacturing, managing compliance is not just a regulatory requirement but a cornerstone of operational integrity and market trust. Compliance requirements state that manufacturing processes adhere to stringent quality standards and regulatory mandates, while also maintaining the agility needed to respond to market changes and technological advancements. By leveraging real-time data analytics, healthcare manufacturers can monitor and analyze every facet of their operations, from supply chain logistics to production line efficiency, ensuring that compliance is woven into the fabric of their operational processes. This approach not only mitigates risks but also enhances decision-making, enabling CIOs to uphold the highest standards of quality and compliance.

Compliance Mastery: BI Tools to Navigate Complex Regulations Effortlessl

Δ Introduction

In the highly regulated medical device manufacturing industry, compliance is not just a requirement but a cornerstone of operational integrity and patient safety. A mid-sized company, with annual revenues between $50 million and $500 million, faced significant challenges in ensuring their high-compliance devices met global standards like HIPAA, HICERT, GDPR, and others. The complexity of adhering to standards such as CFR Part 11 and maintaining General Quality Policy documentation including IQ, OQ, and PQ was overwhelming.

Δ Challenges

The company's journey to compliance mastery was fraught with obstacles:

- **Lack of Visibility:** Difficulty in tracking and documenting compliance across global operations.
- **Complex Regulatory Requirements:** Struggling to keep up with the evolving landscape of HIPAA, HICERT, GDPR, and more.
- **Inefficient Process Monitoring:** Inability to identify and rectify compliance gaps in real time.

- Documentation and Data Gaps: Challenges in maintaining comprehensive and accessible documentation for audits.

Δ Solution

To navigate these challenges, the company implemented a robust solution centered around Real-time Business Intelligence (BI) tools, cloud solutions, and advanced analytics:

- Cloud Solutions and Data Warehousing: By adopting cloud-based solutions and following Ralph Kimball's dimensional modeling best practices, the company ensured scalable, flexible, and efficient data management. This foundational step enabled the aggregation and analysis of compliance-related data across various dimensions.
- Real-time BI Tools: The deployment of real-time BI tools allowed for continuous monitoring of compliance data, alerting management to potential issues, and identifying gaps in data capture and process adherence. These tools provided a comprehensive view of compliance across product lines, groups, categories, and operational locations.
- Advanced Analytics and Machine Learning: Leveraging generative AI, RAG models, predictive and prescriptive analytics, and machine learning,

the company could predict potential compliance risks and automate the generation of compliance scores for various aspects of the operation. This proactive approach enabled timely interventions and continuous improvement.

- **Security and Governance Tools:** To safeguard sensitive data and ensure regulatory compliance, the company implemented state-of-the-art security and governance tools, aligning with global standards and protecting against data breaches.

Δ Benefits

The strategic implementation of these solutions yielded significant benefits:

- **Enhanced Compliance Visibility:** Real-time monitoring and analytics provided a clear, continuous view of compliance status across the organization, reducing the risk of violations.
- **Improved Operational Efficiency:** Automated alerts and predictive analytics helped streamline compliance processes, making it easier to maintain standards and reduce manual oversight.
- **Reduced Risk of Non-Compliance:** The ability to preemptively identify and address compliance gaps significantly lowered the risk of regulatory

penalties and enhanced the company's reputation for reliability and safety.

Δ Summary

For the mid-sized medical device manufacturer, achieving compliance mastery was a transformative journey. By leveraging real-time BI tools, cloud solutions, and advanced analytics, the company not only overcame the complexities of global regulatory requirements but also established a proactive, data-driven approach to compliance monitoring. This strategic initiative not only safeguarded the company against compliance risks but also positioned it as a leader in operational excellence and patient safety. Through this case study, it's clear that with the right technology and strategic focus, navigating the maze of compliance can be turned from a challenge into a competitive advantage.

- **Best Practices for Data Governance at Scale**

As businesses grow and handle more data, implementing strong data governance practices becomes crucial to ensure data quality, security, and compliance. Data governance at scale involves setting clear policies and procedures for how data is collected, stored, accessed, and used across the organization. Think of it as the rules of the road for managing traffic in a bustling city; without them, chaos ensues. Key practices include establishing a dedicated team to oversee data governance, creating a centralized data inventory for visibility into all data assets, and defining data standards to maintain consistency. It's also important to implement robust security measures to protect sensitive information and to ensure compliance with relevant regulations. Regular audits and reviews help identify areas for improvement and ensure adherence to governance policies.

By following these best practices, businesses can maximize the value of their data, minimize risks, and build trust with customers and stakeholders, all while scaling their operations effectively.

- **Agile Methodologies in Large-scale BI**

Implementing Agile methodologies in large-scale Business Intelligence (BI) projects is like navigating a fast-moving river with a skilled team of rafters. This approach emphasizes flexibility, rapid delivery, and close collaboration within teams and with stakeholders, ensuring that BI solutions evolve in response to changing business needs. In an Agile environment, BI projects are broken down into smaller, manageable chunks called sprints, allowing teams to focus on delivering specific features or improvements in short cycles. This method enables quick adjustments based on feedback, reducing the risk of investing in features that don't meet the business's needs. Regular meetings and progress reviews keep everyone aligned and focused on the ultimate goal: creating a BI system that is not only robust and scalable but also adaptable to the dynamic business landscape.

By adopting Agile methodologies, organizations can enhance their BI capabilities more efficiently and effectively, ensuring they remain competitive in an ever-changing market.

Δ Summary

In this chapter, we've traversed the path of scaling your BI initiatives. Like a tree that grows from a sapling to a mighty oak, we've explored how to expand your BI capabilities while keeping the roots firm in agility and quality. By expanding your BI capabilities with a focus on scalability, you are writing the next chapters of your business's success story. Each step, from assessing your current state to implementing scalable solutions and maintaining quality, is a strategic move towards a future-proof narrative that captivates and leads to triumph.

Points to Remember

- A thorough assessment of your current BI infrastructure sets the stage for effective scaling.
- Deciding between incremental growth and significant leaps in BI is crucial and situational.
- The cloud is a powerful ally in the quest for BI scalability.
- Data governance and agile methodologies are the guiding principles as you scale.
- Learning from others' successes provides a map for your own journey of growth.

As we have seen, scaling your BI initiatives is a delicate balance. Next, we'll navigate the future challenges that await on the horizon.

The story of your BI does not end here. As your business grows, new challenges and adventures lie ahead, and our next chapter will prepare you to meet them with confidence and strategy.

Chapter-9

Navigating Future Challenges

This chapter delves into the future of Business Intelligence (BI), emphasizing the importance of foresight, innovation, and strategic agility. We embark on a journey to not only encounter the future but to actively mold it, utilizing our knowledge, anticipatory skills, and innovative spirit.

It's about not just facing the future but shaping it with our own hands, armed with knowledge, anticipation, and the will to innovate.

1. Emerging Trends in BI

The horizon of BI is ever-expanding, with new stars appearing to guide the way. Let's see how.

Δ *Artificial Intelligence and Machine Learning Integration*

The fusion of Artificial Intelligence (AI) and Machine Intelligence (MI) with BI tools is revolutionizing how businesses analyze data, predict trends, and make decisions. This integration allows for more sophisticated data analysis techniques, including predictive analytics, natural language processing, and automated insights generation, making BI tools more powerful and intuitive than ever before.

Δ *Data Quality using AI (DQM)*

In an era where data is the currency, ensuring its quality is of the utmost importance. The use of AI in Data Quality Management (DQM) marks a significant shift towards more automated and efficient processes. By leveraging sophisticated AI algorithms, organizations can now automatically cleanse, validate, and standardize vast amounts of data with unprecedented speed and accuracy. This not only enhances the reliability of Business Intelligence (BI) insights but also significantly reduces the manual effort involved in data preparation, allowing businesses to focus on strategic decision-making based on trustworthy data.

Δ *Data Visualization and Interactive Dashboards*

The trend towards more dynamic and interactive data visualizations continues to grow. Modern BI tools now offer more intuitive and visually appealing dashboards that allow users to interact with their data in real time, enabling more effective data exploration and storytelling. Generative

AI is helping this shift by writing prompts to generate visualization on top of the data cleaned and transformed in a presentable format e.g. Dimensional Data Models.

Δ *Cloud-based BI Solutions*

Cloud-based BI solutions are becoming increasingly popular due to their scalability, flexibility, and cost-effectiveness. These platforms allow businesses of all sizes to access powerful BI capabilities without the need for significant upfront investment in hardware and infrastructure.

Δ *Real-time BI Solutions*

The demand for real-time analytics is driving the development of BI tools that can provide immediate insights. This enables businesses to make faster, data-driven decisions in response to rapidly changing market conditions.

Δ *Augmented BI Solutions*

Augmented analytics uses AI and machine learning to automate the analysis process, making it easier for users to gain insights without deep technical expertise. This trend is democratizing data analysis, making it accessible to a broader range of users within an organization.

Δ *Collaborative BI Solutions*

Collaborative BI tools are designed to enhance teamwork and decision-making by allowing users to share data insights and collaborate on reports and dashboards in real time. This trend is fostering a more data-driven culture within organizations, where insights and decisions are shared across teams and departments.

Δ *Data Privacy and Security*

With increasing amounts of sensitive data being analyzed and stored by BI tools, data privacy and security remain a top priority. Emerging trends in this area focus on implementing more robust security measures, including advanced encryption techniques and access controls, to protect against data breaches and ensure compliance with data protection regulations.

Δ *Self-service BI*

Self-service BI tools are designed to be user-friendly, enabling non-technical users to create reports, analyze data, and generate insights without relying on IT departments. This trend is empowering more users to leverage BI tools, leading to a more informed and agile organization.

Δ *Edge Computing for BI*

Edge computing is emerging as a solution for processing data closer to its source, reducing latency and bandwidth use. In BI, this means faster insights from data generated by IoT devices and other edge sources, enabling more timely and efficient decision-making.

Incorporating these emerging trends into your BI strategy can significantly enhance your organization's analytical capabilities, ensuring you remain at the forefront of data-driven decision-making in today's rapidly evolving business environment.

2. Anticipating and Preparing for Challenges

With new frontiers come new challenges, and the BI landscape is no different. Let's embrace it.

Δ *Bracing for the Unseen*

- ➢ **Data Privacy and Security Concerns:** In our quest for data, we must also guard against threats to privacy and security, ensuring our data treasures are well-protected against potential breaches.
- ➢ **Overcoming Technical Debt in BI Tools:** Legacy systems and outdated methodologies act as anchors, dragging down progress. Innovating and upgrading are essential for breaking free from these constraints.

3. Staying Ahead of the Curve

To stay ahead, we must be the authors of our own BI narratives. Let me explain how.

Δ *Continuous Learning in BI*

The landscape of Business Intelligence (BI) is constantly evolving, necessitating a commitment to lifelong learning and skill enhancement to stay relevant and competitive. With the rapid advancement of technologies and methodologies in BI, professionals and organizations alike must embrace a culture of continuous learning to keep pace with the latest tools, techniques, and best practices.

This ongoing quest for knowledge not only ensures that BI strategies remain cutting-edge but also empowers individuals to innovate and adapt to new challenges, fostering a dynamic and forward-thinking BI community.

The landscape of BI is constantly evolving, necessitating a commitment to lifelong learning and skill enhancement to stay relevant and competitive.

Δ *Building a Culture of Innovation*

Cultivating an environment where innovation is not just welcomed but expected is crucial for driving change and setting new industry standards.

In the realm of Business Intelligence, fostering a culture of innovation means encouraging creative problem-solving, experimentation, and the exploration of new ideas without fear of failure.

This approach not only leads to breakthroughs in BI technologies and practices but also creates a vibrant ecosystem where continuous improvement is the norm, ensuring that organizations not only adapt to the ever-changing business landscape but also lead the way in redefining it.

Δ Summary

This chapter serves as a compass, guiding us through the evolving landscape of Business Intelligence (BI). By delving into the emerging trends, bracing for the forthcoming challenges, and cultivating an ethos of perpetual learning and innovation. It lays out a roadmap for BI practitioners to anticipate shifts, adapt strategies, and embrace continuous evolution, ensuring we remain at the helm of technological advancement and strategic foresight in the realm of BI.

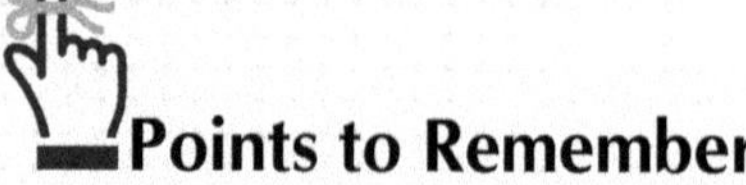

Points to Remember

- The landscape of BI is continually evolving with AI and ML leading the charge.
- Predictive analytics is becoming a vital tool in preempting market shifts.
- Challenges in data privacy and technical debt must be addressed to advance.
- Continuous learning and innovation are the lifeblood of future BI success.

Having explored the forthcoming challenges in Business Intelligence, the time has arrived to concentrate on our ongoing development and education in this domain.

As we turn the page on this chapter, we look towards fostering a perpetual cycle of learning and innovation, ensuring that the BI strategies we implement today will stand the test of time and tide.

Chapter-10

Continuing Your BI Journey

"Putting your resources into acquiring knowledge yields the highest returns."

This sentiment lies at the heart of our ongoing journey in business intelligence—a journey that demands continuous learning and the courage to adapt and innovate.

Far from concluding, this chapter marks a gateway to new horizons in your BI odyssey, urging you to venture further, dive deeper, and reach higher.

1. The Importance of Continuous Learning

Knowledge is infinite, and the landscape is constantly enriched with fresh insights. Please follow these steps for continuous learning.

- **Embrace the Evolution:** Stay at the forefront of BI by continuously exploring emerging technologies, methodologies, and insights that push the boundaries of what's possible.

- **Chart Your Growth:** Design your trajectory in this dynamic field with clear objectives, seeking out mentors and engaging in professional development to enhance your skills and expertise.
- **Inspiration Through Learning:** Let the journey of a BI pioneer, who elevated their expertise through the relentless pursuit of knowledge, motivate you to never stop learning.

2. Adapting to Change

Change is the catalyst for growth, an element that takes you through the transformative journey. Please follow these steps:

- **Seize the Opportunity:** Approach each new development in BI as an open door to innovation, allowing you to reshape and enrich your strategies.
- **Stay Agile:** Keep your strategies flexible, ready to evolve with the shifting tides of the BI landscape, ensuring resilience and relevance.
- **A Tale of Transformation:** Be guided by the story of a company that, by embracing change, steered its course towards uncharted success, setting a benchmark for adaptability.

3. Fostering a Culture of Innovation

Foster a culture where innovation thrives, a realm where every idea has the potential to spark transformation. Here are some ways:

- **Cultivate Creativity:** Foster an environment that champions experimentation, where every team member is empowered to explore, innovate, and contribute to the BI journey.
- **Reward Ingenuity:** Recognize and celebrate the trailblazers who bring fresh perspectives and novel solutions, infusing your BI narrative with vibrant, new colors.
- **Adventures in Innovation:** Draw inspiration from a team of BI explorers who dared to venture beyond the known, transforming their workspace into a landscape of endless possibilities and discoveries.

Δ Summary

As we conclude this chapter, remember: the journey of BI is ever-unfolding and rich with potential for those who dare to pursue it. Armed with the insights from this playbook, you're poised to navigate the evolving world of BI, driving your story forward with knowledge, agility, and a pioneering spirit. Let's embrace this endless path of discovery, shaping the future of business intelligence together.

Please don't forget the power of lifelong learning and the pursuit of innovation in the dynamic world of Data and AI aka Business Intelligence through AI innovation. It is an invitation to continue writing your story, to keep learning and growing, and to stay ever-curious and bold on the path of Real-Time Business Intelligence (BI) Mastery.

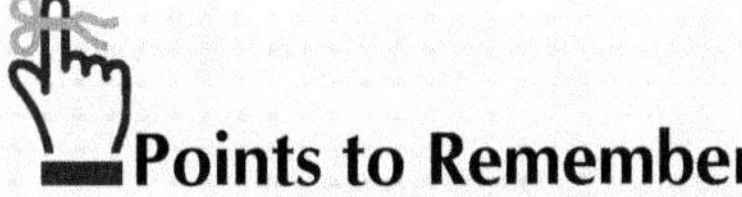

Points to Remember

- Continuous learning is essential for staying relevant in the ever-evolving BI field.
- Adapting to change is necessary for the longevity and success of your BI initiatives.
- A culture of innovation is the fertile soil from which a robust BI strategy grows.

As we wrap up the book, equipped with the necessary resources, strategies, and motivation to further your Business Intelligence path, this is where we encapsulate our journey and share our parting insights into the evolving landscape of Real-Time Business Intelligence.

As we draw this playbook to a close, we look back only to see how far we've come—and then we turn forward, eyes on the horizon, ready for the next chapter in our BI adventure.

Conclusion

Leading the Future with Real Time BI

Every story ends with what effectively marks a fresh start, and within the realm of Business Intelligence, this concluding segment acts as your bridge to the future.

Δ Recap

As we reflect on the journey this book has taken us on, let's revisit the key milestones that have shaped our understanding and strategy:

- **Building the Foundation:** We began by laying the groundwork, understanding the critical role of data in modern manufacturing, and setting the stage for a transformative shift towards a data-centric approach in all facets of business operations.
- **The 5-Step Playbook:** Through the playbook, we navigated the intricacies of real-time business intelligence, from harnessing automation and streamlining operations to fostering a culture ripe

for data-driven decision-making, each step a tactical move towards achieving unparalleled operational excellence.

- **Beyond the Playbook:** Looking ahead, we explored the strategies that extend beyond the foundational playbook, anticipating future trends, adapting to evolving challenges, and continuously pushing the boundaries of innovation to remain at the forefront of the manufacturing industry in an ever-changing landscape.

This book presents an innovative approach, combining the powerful capabilities of Real-Time Business Intelligence with the anticipation ability of Artificial Intelligence.

It's not just a repository of information but provides you with a playbook on how to execute the strategy and take your organization to 10x profits, stability, and growth. This book outlines how real-time BI and AI are not just tools but game-changers.

It's about utilizing real-time data not just to respond to market demands, but to predict, anticipate and lead them. The book is designed to instruct you on cultivating a data-centric mindset, training your employees, and choosing the right Data and AI tools that turn data into a prime resource.

Take the first step into a future where your manufacturing business doesn't just thrive - it leads.

Δ Looking Ahead

- **The AI Horizon:** AI is no longer just an ally; it's becoming a part of the BI fabric, woven into every aspect of data analysis and decision-making.
- **The Next Wave of Innovation:** As the tides of technology rise, so do the opportunities for those ready to sail these waters with an eye for the horizons of tomorrow.

Δ Final Words of Encouragement

- **The Journey Continues:** This playbook is just the beginning. The real story unfolds as you take these strategies and weave them into the fabric of your business.
- **Embrace the Challenge:** The road ahead is filled with both opportunities and obstacles, but with the playbook in hand, you are more than equipped to navigate it.

Your journey towards data mastery and unprecedented business growth starts here.

We close this playbook not with a full stop, but with an ellipsis... an invitation to continue writing your story, to keep turning the pages, and to lead the future with the power of Real-Time Business Intelligence.

Continue Your Journey With Me.......

Δ Plan Your Strategic Meeting

Kickstart your journey towards transforming your manufacturing operation with a personalized strategic discussion. Don't fall behind the competition - arrange a meeting with our experienced professionals today. Together, we will chart out the plan for your organization's success using Real-Time Business Intelligence and AI. Your future as an industry leader starts with this conversation.

Unlock Your Manufacturing Potential. Schedule a Consultation Now

- https://bit.ly/meet dave goyal

Δ Free Audit

Get Your Free Data (BI and DW) and AI Audit - The Foundation for Growth. Discover your data's hidden potential. Secure your free audit today to uncover valuable insights and opportunities within your current operations.

Our comprehensive audit is the first move towards a leaner, more agile, and data-driven manufacturing environment.

We are giving you this assessment at zero cost and no obligation as we believe it could trigger your next stage of growth and help your executive team understand why you need it.

Schedule your free audit now.

➢ https://bit.ly/getyourfeeaudit

❖ ❖ ❖ ❖

∆ Download the Blueprint

Get the Blueprint – A Guide to Success Driven by Real-Time Data and AI. Start your journey to data excellence with our exclusive blueprint designed for future manufacturing leaders. This is your road map for integrating Real-Time BI and AI into your operations' core. Don't miss the chance to transform your decision-making process and operational efficiency using this guide.

As a thank you from me for patiently reading through this book, please download the blueprint and start shaping a future where data insights lead to decisive action.

Download now and begin crafting your future where data insights lead to definitive action.

➢ https://bit.ly/RTBIBlueprint

❖ ❖ ❖ ❖

www.ingramcontent.com/pod-product-compliance
Ingram Content Group UK Ltd.
Pitfield, Milton Keynes, MK11 3LW, UK
UKHW021659190726
13853UKWH00001B/350

9 789355 549594